Motherhood is a divine  about Himself while mor. Erin Hawley is an attent _ joys or what it means for us to be dearly beloved children of the living God. With grace and gentleness, insights and discovery, *Living Beloved* invites mothers to enter into the Sabbath of being beloved. Share this sweet gift with the mothers in your circle of influence.

PeggySue Wells
Mom of seven and bestselling author of 28 titles, including
Bonding with Your Child through Boundaries (with June Hunt)

If you are a mom with young children, put this book by your Bible and read it! If you are a mentor of young moms, use this book in a study with them. If you are a grandmother, give this book to all your daughters! With humor and honesty, Hawley combines biblical stories with real-life mom experiences to give us a treasure chest full of new insights about God's personal love, a fresh awareness of what our children can teach us, and the sweet companionship of a "friend who gets me!"

Susan Alexander Yates
Speaker and author of *And Then I Had Kids: Encouragement for Mothers of Young Children* and *Character Matters! Raising Kids with Values That Last*

I believe this beautiful book has the potential to change your life— as it carries a powerful message, not only for mothers, but for every girl with a desire to grow in their understanding of God's amazing love for them.

Debbie Lindell
Lead pastor of James River Church and author of *She Believes*

This is not really a book about parenting as much as it is a book about "child-ing." Filled with personal stories and insightful research, Erin's intelligent writing style captures deep theological truths that will transform how you think of God as your Father. Although written particularly to young mothers, as a pastor I recommend this book for everyone.

Dave Cover
Pastor of The Crossing

By the end of the first page of *Living Beloved*, I was breathing a sigh of relief and solace: *this is a safe place*. There are no comparisons here, or expectations, only an opportunity to find rest and identity in God's grace. Erin weaves the stories of childhood and motherhood truthfully, inviting us tired mamas to remember that we are children, perfectly loved and nurtured by the parent-heart of God.

Catherine McNiel
Author of *Long Days of Small Things: Motherhood as a Spiritual Discipline*

So many of us are moving through this life in "survival mode," just trying our hardest to make it through each day. We've become a generation of do-it-all moms, multitaskers to the max. What a beautiful reminder Erin Hawley has given us to pause, ponder, rest, and purposefully recognize the numerous lessons the Lord wants to reveal to us about Himself and His steadfast love through our children and motherhood.

Julie Manning
Author of *My Heart*

living
Beloved

living
Beloved

*Lessons from my little ones
about the heart of God*

Erin Hawley

TYNDALE HOUSE PUBLISHERS, INC.
CAROL STREAM, ILLINOIS

FOCUS ON THE FAMILY® | FOCUS ON PARENTING™

The use of material from or references to various websites does not imply endorsement of those sites in their entirety. Availability of websites and pages is subject to change without notice.

Editor: Julie Buscho Holmquist

Cover design by Callie Wilburn

Cover photo: © 2018 iStock.com/monkeybusinessimages. All rights reserved.

For information about special discounts for bulk purchases, please contact Tyndale House Publishers at csresponse@tyndale.com, or call 1-800-323-9400.

Library of Congress Cataloging-in-Publication Data can be found at www.loc.gov.

ISBN 978-1-58997-032-8

Printed in the United States of America

24	23	22	21	20	19	18
7	6	5	4	3	2	1

To Elijah and Blaise. The two of you have brought so much joy, laughter, and light into my life. I am so very thankful to be your mom and for the privilege of seeing the childlike in you. I love you.

Contents

Foreword

Living Beloved

I remember with perfect clarity the moment I knew I loved Erin. We were working together at the time—office mates, actually, in a small office with high ceilings and two substantial desks pressed together in the center of the room, facing each other, so that every time I looked up for a year I saw her.

Though it didn't take me a year to know about Erin. We started on the job in early July, and it was an afternoon in the middle fall, maybe October: Our employer, a federal judge, had invited us to join him on a patio outdoors in the autumn sun, and we were gathering up plates and forks and a cherry pie someone had made to take out with us. I had plates in one hand and the pie in another, and as I started toward the door I bobbled the pie. And before I could say a word, Erin instantly, without a second's hesitation, reached out and took my hand.

There was something about that touch. It said something to me in that moment, to my heart—an offer of help, but also of solidarity, of standing together; a touch that said *I'm here when you're weak, I'm here in your need.* I've loved Erin ever since. And cherry pie.

In these pages, Erin comes alongside you to steady, to encourage, to inspire. She shares from her own life what she has learned as a mother about the loving heart of God. And she draws out in ways only a mother can what that mighty love amounts to. She helps us see that God's love invites us to be cherished children, beloved sons and daughters, defined by a passion that beat for us before we were born and makes us all that we are.

I can't help but think, in reading Erin's pages, of the apostle Paul's conviction that God had set him apart "from my mother's womb and called me by his grace." Erin helps us understand how true that is for each of us, loved by God before we have done a thing, loved for who we are as *His*. May the Lord help you experience that love in new ways through these pages.

Erin urges her readers at the outset to take it slow, to allow the Lord space and time to work as you read. I couldn't agree more. Savor every page. Maybe read it with a piece of cherry pie.

Josh Hawley

Introduction

Motherhood has brought me nearly to the end of myself. And for that I will be forever grateful.

The early years felt overwhelming. The math just didn't work. A full-time job squeezed into part-time babysitting hours and a husband with a travel-heavy work schedule added up to not enough hours in the day. As busy days followed sleepless nights, I began to identify with Psalm 79:3's lament, "They have poured out their blood like water all around Jerusalem, and there was no one to bury them." For me, there was no one to bury the aspirations of being a wonderful wife, mom, professor, author, Bible study leader, and friend. No one to bury the need to have it all together, to be the on-top-of-things twenty-first-century wife, mom, and career woman.

As the daughter of an alcoholic, I had long defined my identity by my performance. Through a series of remarkable, only-God-could-do-this events, a small-town girl attended the nation's best law school, worked for its top judge, and participated in cases discussed on the six o'clock news. But I was never sure I was good enough. My response to each new opportunity was to resort to one rule: Work harder.

This self-imposed rule didn't leave a lot of room for me to fail. Nor did it leave much room for the Lord to move in grace and power. As a result, I was unprepared for the reality that is motherhood—where control is beyond one's ken. When my husband was disappointed, or my son cried at being left with the babysitter (or because his stomach hurt or because babies sometimes cry), or when I called to tell the conference organizer that I couldn't make it to speak, the walls closed in. It wasn't possible to work harder to fix things. Oh, believe me, I tried. I walked miles up and down our staircase trying to comfort the acid-reflux stomach of our oldest son, banged out legal articles during nap times, tried to cook *Food and Wine*-worthy dinners, and hosted Bible studies on nights my husband was out of town. But the pieces kept falling. There wasn't enough. *I* wasn't enough.

One tired evening, the thought hit me: God *could* have made motherhood easy. It would have been simple enough for the King of kings to create babies who slept through the night. The God who made the stars might easily have gifted me with intuitive knowledge of how best to deal with a tiny acid-reflux tummy. So if God is good—and I believe He is—and if God is sovereign—and I believe He is—my tired mind wondered, why all the sleepless nights? Why are human babies (in marked contrast to many others in the natural world) so dependent?

C. S. Lewis reminds us that we are never told another's story. Your own motherhood journey has unique God-imprints, sweet whispered love songs to you alone. But for me, the Lord has quietly and steadfastly been showing me that, although little ones might not sleep the night through, the Lord is always there to catch my falling pieces.

Those early months brought me to the end of myself in a way nothing else has, and thus to the beginning of God. The promised grace, the working of all things to the good, the God-plan, was ever so much more wonderful than I could have dreamed, because God was there. He met me at my worst when I was not enough (and still am not) and proved Himself all sufficient.

It was as a mom that the Father God invited me to become a child again—His child. To rediscover, or discover anew, the joy of being fully, unconditionally, and perfectly loved. Through the transition to motherhood—a transition that has not always been easy—I've been given a second chance to become childlike, to rest in God's provision and protection, to dance with joy, and to dream the impossible. My children are teaching me to be comfortable with dependency, to anticipate and wonder and praise and live life all-in. Every day my boys show me what it means to have a childlike spirit and what it is that the Father invites me to become.

I've discovered that part of God's grand plan for me as a mom is to see my children as He created them—with all of their joy, exuberance, trust, desire for relationship, and ability to rest. In the Bible, Jesus talks a lot about children, which is surprising when you consider that children had no place in society at the time. Jesus upends all of that. Instead of being the least and the last, children are the chosen, the first in, the ones Jesus time and again welcomes with outstretched arms.

Children are important to Jesus, and not just because the God of the universe uniquely designs each one, but because they possess and reveal the characteristics of the Kingdom. Jesus, in other words, not only adores children, He teaches that to inherit the Kingdom of Heaven we must *become like them*.

When the disciples were arguing over who among them would be the greatest in the Kingdom of Heaven, Jesus did something shocking. He called a small child to Himself and upended the disciples' world. Jesus said, "Let the little children come to me and do not hinder them, for to such belongs the kingdom of heaven" (Matthew 19:14). One like this—this small, humble child, Jesus explained—will be the greatest in the Kingdom of Heaven. Indeed, becoming childlike is the key to entering heaven in the first place: Jesus told His disciples, "Truly, I say to you, unless you turn and become like children, you will never enter the kingdom of heaven" (Matthew 18:3).

As moms, we have a ringside seat to the heavenly characteristics Jesus emphasized to the disciples. Through a haze of tiredness, we receive an unexpected and priceless gift: By focusing on the unique attributes of our children, we see how God created them *and us* to be. That is, when we see our children as Jesus saw them, we see the very characteristics that the Lord desires to see in us. And as we become childlike, we learn to embrace our identity and live fully from a place of adoption—adoption as beloved children of the Father God.

Now, a brief note is necessary to point out what every mom knows: Children are *not* perfect. They learn "no" and "mine" at a very early age and often behave like tiny dictators. It's even been said that two hundred toddlers could conquer the world. (Personally, I think that number may be too high.) When Jesus speaks of the Kingdom of Heaven being made up of children, He isn't talking about childishness but the natural, spontaneous traits of very young children.

Children, for example, don't work at being children. They just are. And this is important. Being childlike means *becoming* more without *doing* more. Our children show us how. In their desire just to be with Mom, they show us how to lean up into a relationship with Jesus. In finding their identity in their parents, they show us that the key to identity is not inward introspection but outward focus on our Father. They risk and they trust and they are

transparent—sometimes all in the same breath. And they do all of
this because they understand who they are in relationship to their
parents.

Of course, children are also unbelievably active. Some days they
don't stop moving—ever. But children are unique in that they act
from a position of being. They make outrageous requests of their
parents. They find joy in every frog, fish, and even dead mole. They
explode in spontaneous expressions of wonder. They show us that
following Jesus actually means being pursued by Him. They rest.
They show us how to actively participate in life by being secure in
love. They act out of a place of being.

Every day my children show me the Father's heart, what He
longs to see in me. As Jesus taught the disciples with parables, the
word pictures of His heart, He has been teaching me in this hard
season of motherhood through those He's entrusted to my care.

Dear one, this book is not a how-to on motherhood. It's a book
for the mom whose memory is foggy, whose patience is fraying,
and who desperately would like a good night's sleep and a peaceful
shower—or at least one of the two. It's for poured-out moms who
desperately need spiritual refreshment. It's about discovering God's
unique and surprising invitation to moms as they go about the vital
but so often exhausting business of nurturing their children.

If the early years of motherhood are challenging for you, I am
right there with you. There have been (and still are) days I have felt
insufficient and depleted. On the most difficult days, God has provided spiritual nourishment from a surprising place: He has taught
me lessons about living as a child of God from my own children.

Through my young boys, God has shown me more of what it means to be His child. Dear ones, I'm so very excited to share with you the ways that seeing my children's childlikeness has encouraged and emboldened me to live as a beloved child of God.

Through your everyday, ordinary task of loving and nurturing your children as no one else can do, the Father God is inviting you to learn from them how to grow closer to Him, how to accept His invitation to be His beloved child. He wants to shower you with grace in the midst of chaos. He wants to refresh and renew you through those He has entrusted to your care. Dear one, hear Him today as He invites you to think of yourself as a child of God in a whole new way.

My prayer is that this book might encourage and refresh you, help you grow closer to the Lord, and enjoy being His beloved child. I pray that this book might nourish and speak to your soul as you nourish and care for your children. It's my hope that the Lord would use this book to affirm you in your motherhood journey, to remind you of His promises and your identity as a daughter of God. Most of all, I pray that as you snuggle your own children close, you'd feel the Father's arms around you, assuring you of His love.

Dear one, I urge you to take this book slowly as you study your children. Read it in bits and pieces when you can manage between the dishes and the diapers, and ask God the Father to show you the lessons He has to teach you through your children.

1

Humble Imitation

*Therefore be imitators of God [copy Him and
follow His example], as well-beloved children
[imitate their father]. And walk in love.*

—Ephesians 5:1-2, AMPC

Elijah's three-year-old legs pump as hard as they can go, his head is flung back, and his hair blows in the breeze. His breath comes in audible, hard rushes. He looks like he's running the last ten meters of a two-hundred-meter dash or perhaps running for his life. Every ounce of energy, every fiber of his being, is stretched to the breaking.

I imagine the crossing of a finish line, the breaking of a taut ribbon, the victory dance. But instead of victory, there's a miscarriage of hope. Elijah gradually slows, from full-on irrepressible run to timid trot and, finally, to a dejected walk with his head hanging down. Then his feet stop moving entirely. He's motionless; his goal is beyond reach, his dreams crushed, and his heart broken. It's the three-year-old version of locusts and ashes.

You see, Elijah was not chasing after a blue ribbon but rather stretched out in pursuit of his father. My husband, Josh, was running his three miles on our long driveway. Up and back. Up and back. Up and back. We were playing outside when Elijah saw his daddy run past and wanted to run with him. He wanted to be doing just what he saw his father doing.

The sight was beautiful and heartbreaking. As hard as he tried, Elijah was unable to run as far or as fast as his dad. His lungs were too small and his feet too slow. His body failed him, his efforts insufficient.

But then from around the bend came Josh. Seeing the tears flooding down Elijah's face, he scooped him up and ran a few hundred yards with him in his arms. Tears of sadness turned to tears of joy. The run with the father was sweeter because it was unexpected; the arms that held the boy dearer because of his own failure; the closeness cherished even more because *it was all grace.* It was just when hope was lost, and a small heart thought its desire was out of reach, that the father reached down to turn heartache into relationship.

How like our heavenly Father. It is often when night seems darkest that our Father God's pursuit of us becomes clear and real. It's in the hour of defeat. It's when we break off from running, our feet motionless and our heads hanging down, feeling discouraged and disillusioned. It's when our efforts and our intellect and our stubbornness run out. It's when we need God—when we acknowledge that need to ourselves and to Him.

It's *then* that our Father makes His presence known. He picks us up and holds us close with arms full of strength and grace and forgiveness. He delights in us. He upholds us. And our tears turn to joy. Our ashes turn to beauty and our mourning to dancing. He redeems the years the locusts have eaten (Joel 2:25). He renews our strength. He promises that those who hope in the Lord will run and never grow weary (Isaiah 40:31).

Our children are constantly imitating us. In their unselfconscious desire to be like us, their moms, we see Ephesians 5:1-2 lived out. We see what it means to be "imitators of God"; it's living as beloved children, children who copy their parents. As imitators, children also show us that the one who loves us is nearby and always pursuing us. They teach us that following Jesus means radical freedom and that, when we follow and humbly imitate Jesus, we're surrounded by love on every side. Let's explore each of these ideas in turn.

PURSUED FOLLOWERS

I watch in awe as my two-and-a-half-year-old mimics my morning contact routine down to the last idiosyncrasy. He opens the contact case and takes out a pretend contact. He rinses the clean contact with solution—never you mind that it's been sitting in fresh solution all night. He peers up into the mirror, a move made more difficult by the fact that he's standing on the sink counter. He scrutinizes his face critically, pries open his right eye, and gently pops in the contact. I am speechless. I had no idea Elijah had been watching my morning routine, let alone so closely. He was beyond excited to be doing something big, to be doing something that I do, and to be doing it just the way I did.

My awe turns to dismay as I realize how closely those little eyes have been watching. Every small moment is one of impact when the eyes that see have yet to turn three. Little eyes watch to see how I react to the slow grocery-store line or to the service representative on the other end of the phone. Impressionable eyes observe the way I drive, the way I talk to my own mom, and the food (including massive amounts of Diet Dr Pepper) that I put in my body. I desperately want to be a good example.

Then a bigger realization hits even closer to home. Do I seek to emulate the person who I'm supposed to be becoming like? Am I living out the Ephesians 5:1-2 exhortation to be an imitator of God, to copy Him and follow His example, *as beloved children imitate their own* parents?

Jesus is spotless. He is righteousness. His loving-kindness knows no end. His Spirit reveals His character, one of "love, joy, peace, patience, kindness, goodness, faithfulness, gentleness, self-control" (Galatians 5:22-23). The entire universe was created by Him and through Him and for Him (Romans 11:36). And somehow we are supposed to become like Him, as Paul said he did in 1 Corinthians 11:1. We are to follow in Jesus' steps (1 Peter 2:21) and to have His attitude and mind-set (Philippians 2:3-8).

But am I living this? Am I imitating Him as a beloved child? Do I begin my day studying Jesus, as my two-year-old clearly studies me? Do I see, really see, how He loves people, how He approaches the unapproachable, how He gives away grace, always? Do I see the patience with which the Lord treats the Israelites? Time and again they rebel, yet the Lord continually pursues them with His "never stopping, never giving up, unbreaking, always and forever love."[1] Or am I too busy? Too distracted? My son desperately wants to become like me. Do I desperately want to become like Jesus?

The answer is painfully clear. No. Not always. Not often, even. There's certainly a place for my heartfelt prayer, "Lord, help me to be more like You; Lord, help me to *want* to be like You."

But as I watch my children, I realize that even as Jesus calls us to follow Him, He's pursuing us. Our relationship is all grace. Even the imitation and the following are more about Jesus than about me. Jesus is the author and perfecter of our faith. He draws us close and enables both our desire and our transformation. Jesus promises to be with us, to give us new hearts, and to keep working in us until He returns. We *are* His workmanship.

You see, Elijah's morning contact routine was made possible only with my support. My arms held him close, preventing a tumble from the bathroom sink and enabling his imitation. Elijah's imitation was facilitated by me, his mom. The same thing is true of our imitation of Jesus. When we seek to follow Him, He pursues us. It's God the Father, God the Son, and God the Holy Spirit holding us close, supporting us, enabling us, sustaining us, giving us life and breath and all. As we take a step to follow His example, we can be confident that He is with us.

And during the times when we fail, or the times when we fail to begin, the Father comes close and runs with us. He scoops us up and holds us close. It's His arms that support and His legs that run the distance. The Father always pursues us.

When Jesus says "Follow me," the disciples do and we should too. But time and again, Jesus makes it clear that He's pursuing us. It was Jesus who continually turned back to shore up and encourage the disciples. Think of Peter walking on water: When fear overwhelmed and the waters rose, it was Jesus who stretched out His arms. When Thomas doubted, it was Jesus who held out His hands and His side. When Peter denied Jesus three times in His hour of greatest need, the risen Lord later sought him and restored him, asking one question—"Simon, son of John, do you love me?" (John 21:15-17)—for each denial. It was Jesus who offered each question as a healing touch on a painful wound.

God pursues us relentlessly. Psalm 23 famously proclaims the truth that the Lord's goodness and mercy shall "follow us" all the days of our lives. But the original Hebrew word used for follow, *radaf*, is much stronger than a passive sort of trailing behind. *Radaf* is a bold, active, life-changing word most often translated as "pursue." Psalm 23 easily could be translated to mean that the Lord's goodness, mercy, and unfailing love shall *pursue* us all the days of our lives. In fact, in *The Message*, Eugene Peterson translates *radaf* as "chase after," telling us that the Lord's goodness, mercy, and love shall *chase after* us every day of our lives.

As we follow Jesus, we realize that we are the ones being pursued. God chases us with an unfailing love—He runs after us with His blessings. He pursues us.

RADICAL FREEDOM

Some of my favorite memories of my children come from when they were knee high. This height was perfect for the "knee check." The boys would career about playing with friends or exploring a new playground, but every so often they would zoom back to me, wrap their arms around my legs in a full body hug, snuggle their faces in my knees. Because Mom's knees were close, my boys were at liberty to explore and discover. They were radically free because of their relationship to their parent—a parent who pursued them should they wander too far. In a similar way, when Jesus invites us to follow Him, when He pursues us, it is then that we are radically free.

There is nothing wishy-washy about Jesus' invitation to the disciples. Mark tells us that when Jesus saw Simon and Andrew fishing in the Sea of Galilee, He said to them, "Follow me, and I will make you become fishers of men" (Mark 1:17). Mark goes on to describe how Simon and Andrew *immediately* left their nets and followed Him. They left their boats, their businesses, and their families. Similarly, when Jesus called Matthew He said simply, "Follow me" (Matthew 9:9). Matthew immediately got up from his tax-collecting booth, "left everything behind" (Luke 5:28, NASB), and began to follow Jesus.

Can we imagine leaving home, vocation, and family on the basis of only two words? "Follow me." Yet there is something so irresistible about Jesus that Simon and Andrew and Matthew did just that, without a moment's hesitation.

All of this does not compare, of course, to what Jesus gave up. As Philippians 2:6-8 reminds us,

> [Jesus], though he was in the form of God, did not count equality with God a thing to be grasped, but emptied himself, by taking the form of a servant, being born in the likeness of men. And being found in human form, he humbled himself by becoming obedient to the point of death, even death on a cross.

And it does not compare to what we receive: abundant life today and eternity with Jesus.

But there is no question that when Jesus calls He asks us to put

Him first. Ironically, this radical notion of loving Jesus more than our own spouses, children, parents, and friends is what enables us to love each of them better. Jesus teaches us what it means to be a better mom, spouse, and friend.

I'm struck not only by how Jesus asks us to put Him first, and thus put everything else second, but also how Jesus invites us to leave behind the baggage that holds us captive. Beth Moore describes a person's captivity as "anything that hinders the abundant and effective Spirit-filled life God planned for him or her."[2] Anything—our pride, our inadequate sense of who we are in Christ, our past, our hurts, the idols we have set up in place of God—anything that hinders us in the life God has called us to has taken us captive no less than prison walls.

But God became man and died on a cross to free us from physical *and* spiritual captivity. Isaiah previews the Messiah, announcing, "Is not this the fast that I choose: to loose the bonds of wickedness, to undo the straps of the yoke, to let the oppressed go free, and to break every yoke?" (Isaiah 58:6). Jesus came to loose our bonds, to set the oppressed free, and to break *every* tie that binds.

In following Jesus, then, we leave behind those things that yoke us to sin and death and keep us from living fully the life He has called us to. No matter how deep or old or secret the wounds, Jesus invites us to lay them at His feet. As counterintuitive as it sounds, following Jesus means radical freedom.

❧

I was about eight years old, and my sisters and I were on our way to Grandmom's house—a place I knew I didn't belong. Because, well, Grandmom's house was *normal*. There was no screaming. Chairs were not overturned, dishes did not crash against walls, and pickup trucks did not flip after one drink too many. I knew what to expect at Grandmom's house: laughter, enormous meals, and relief from the constant worry that any small incident, any out-of-place word, or even some good intention might result in the latest breakdown of family harmony that showed up in angry words, swift punishment, and, worst of all, the oft-made accusation that we three children did not love our father.

Even though Grandmom's house was blissfully predictable and safe, our weekly visits were fraught with peril. I knew deep in my being that I did not belong in a place like this and that, if I was found out, I might not be invited back.

As a child of an alcoholic, I had developed a keen, unhealthy attention to the emotions of those around me. While my maternal grandparents loved us dearly, my sisters and I were quite aware of the tension between extended family members. My parents' marriage had not been easy. My dad suffered from alcoholism and severe depression—diseases that often left him incapable of being a loving husband and father. Try as he might, he could not get better, and home life got progressively worse.

During my parents' twelve-year marriage, I can remember only one time that Grandmom visited our house (Granddad never came, to my knowledge). That single visit ended memorably when Dad screaming at Grandmom. She left in tears. And she never came back.

Thus, "going to Grandmom's house" evoked many emotions. Some of my happiest childhood memories are of the extended family gathered around her huge dining-room table, relatives crowded together, laughing. The food was wonderful, the cousins plentiful, and the fights nonexistent. The house was an oasis of peace and consistency for three girls who were used to the upheaval and chaos that accompany alcoholism.

The differences between our home and Grandmom's home were palpable: My sisters and I could *feel* the difference. To me, the gaping gulf between the normal and the chaotic was so large it was impassible. This perception led to my own sneaking suspicion that, even at Grandmom's house, everyone was looking for signs of errancy, waiting for us to turn out badly. I felt as if I were on probation, an interloper in that happy place, and so very fearful of discovery.

As a result, I was determined to be the best kid possible. To my eight-year-old mind, that meant washing dishes. So before the meal was complete, I would jump up from the table and begin clearing it. I'd fill the sink, scrape the plates into the trash, and scrub. Behind the mound of dishes was a small girl looking for some sign of approval, an acknowledgment that my sisters and I could stay. That we belonged. I can remember watching my uncle lean back in his chair, laughing, while I wished for the quiet confidence that it would take to sit back and enjoy the meal, to linger over dessert, to simply *be*.

Simply *being* was not enough in my family. It was not enough for my dad, who could not see love through the fog of alcohol and depression. It was not enough for the little girl who was so very desperate for unconditional love that she scrambled to receive approval for washing dishes, of all things. And it was not enough (still sometimes is not enough) for the adult me, who still longs to belong, who often works at the task set before her with a frenzy born not of desire but of fear.

I didn't think being me was enough for the Lord, either. In *Blue Like Jazz*, Donald Miller writes eloquently about the difficulty of knowing a loving heavenly Father when our relationships with our earthly fathers are difficult. I knew John 3:16 by heart, that the Lord had sent His Son, His only Son, to die on the cross that we might have everlasting life. And I believed. Yet while I believed that the Lord had made the ultimate sacrifice, I didn't see Him in the day-to-day of childhood. Family life—from my dad's unshakeable conviction that I didn't love him, to his unpredictable behavior and harsh words, to his final decision to take his own life—was difficult to reconcile with a God who sees the details. I knew God not as a loving Father but as a sovereign, all-powerful, and yet unreachable God.

It's taken me a long time to understand that simply being *is* enough for Jesus. He doesn't lose His temper when the pieces fall. No plates crash and no angry words are exchanged. In fact, when we fail, Jesus is not even disappointed in us but sees in us His own hard-won righteousness. He meets us in our brokenness. He sees us and feels with us. He not only looks down from on high and loves us, but He gets down in the trenches with us. He pursues us.

And He wants us to lay the things that bind down at His feet. He wants us to follow *Him* and lose *them*. As *The Message* paraphrase of John 3:16 puts it, "This is how much God loved the world: He gave his Son, his one and only Son. And this is why: so that no one need be destroyed; by believing in him, anyone *can have a whole and lasting life*" (emphasis mine). Jesus sacrificed so much so that we might have a "whole and lasting life." Even today, that phrase brings me to tears. He doesn't want us just to survive, to wade through the long days, trying to avoid as much pain as possible. He doesn't want us to grow brittle shells or present a perfectly coifed imposter to the world.

He wants us to *live*. Fully and wholly. Abundantly. And we can because He came to loose every bond as we follow Him. Even if your family looks something like mine or is unbearably difficult in some other heartbreaking way, hear me say this: Jesus cares. He is with you now and He was with you then. When Jesus says "Follow me," He's inviting us to follow Him and to lose those things that imprison us. In following Jesus, there's radical freedom.

Surrounded by Love

I'm reminded of my two-year-old, Blaise, sitting under a tangle of blankets on top of the couch. We were playing peekaboo as I multitasked putting laundry away and watching his older brother in the bath. Finally, Blaise got tired of having one-third of my attention. As I peeked my head in the room, he pulled back a blanket, patted the couch, and said, "Come sit with me in the piles." And you know what? This mama did. I left the laundry, got Elijah out of the bath, sat down "in the piles" with my two-year-old, and pulled him close.

Dear sister, how much more will our Father God sit with us in our piles and pull us close? The Lord doesn't run from our mess; He embraces us in it. We don't scare the Lord. He loves to come and sit with us in our piles. All we have to do is pat the couch and ask. And when we do, we find that He is already there.

"I am with you always," promises Jesus (Matthew 28:20). And He is. His light is what makes the darkness bearable. But this isn't a promise of a trouble-free life. In fact, Isaiah 43:2's famous promise that the Lord will be with us when we pass through the waters *assumes* that through waters we *shall* pass. Nor is it that we will understand everything once we put our faith in Jesus. The Bible tells us that there are some things we will not understand this side of heaven. But we can be certain that we are never alone. God the Father is the one who sees us always, Jesus the Son became man because of His overwhelming compassion for us, and the Holy Spirit lives within us comforting us and advocating for us at every turn.

For me personally, I may never know why some things happened, but I do know that I was not alone. It took me years to face some of the hard things about my childhood. Through my church's healing prayer ministry, however, Jesus showed me a vision that changed everything. As I prayed, I saw Grandmom's kitchen clearly, as if I were there in the moment.

The double sink below the wide window looks out into a flower garden and a small fruit-tree orchard beyond. The Formica countertops are piled high with dishes, the fancy ones reserved for holidays. The island overflows with food. The dining table stretches out nearby, its leaves extended to accommodate the large gathering. Family members are sitting, laughing, lingering over dessert and coffee.

There's a skinny blonde girl at the sink. She's washing dishes. Alone. But suddenly she's not sad anymore. And she's not alone. The sink is overflowing bubbles, and a little boy, not much older and not any bigger than the girl, is washing dishes too. They are up to their elbows in soapsuds. Dishwater splashes high as four arms—not a lonely single pair—plunge into the soapy water. Their eyes are full of laughter, and as sunlit faces turn, I know it's Jesus, come to wash dishes with a tiny little girl.

Jesus knew my little-girl heart, my feelings of inadequacy, and my desperate desire to belong. He knew the fear that drove me to wash dishes before dessert was finished, and He met me there. He was beside me washing dishes too and delighting in me. While I might have worried about fitting in with my family, He was telling me that I belonged to Him. There was nothing I could do that would make Him love me any more or any less. I could simply *be*.

This example may seem fantastical, but for me it is a picture of the truth that Jesus never forsakes us. The vision helped me to see that He was with me all along—protecting, loving, laughing even, with the little girl I was. For me, Jesus makes every memory bearable, beautiful even, because He's in every one.

Jesus sees, and He cares about the little things. He cares about the small girl who doesn't belong, and He cares about you. Dear friend, I pray that Jesus' love would envelop you. I pray that you would see His hands and feet at work in your life right now, and that if you have memories that are difficult to bear, Jesus would reveal Himself to you there too. He is there.

As we follow Jesus, He surrounds us.

We were visiting with friends who had children just a few years older than ours. Our oldest was still sleeping peacefully, so we enjoyed story after story about their eldest child's ability to escape from crib and room (little knowing we were hearing our future). The mom recounted their solution: a baby monitor with a two-way speaker. When their son popped up and began climbing out of his crib again, his mom spoke sternly into the monitor: "Get back into bed." The poor little guy had no idea that his mother could see him, much less that she could speak out of thin air, and was nearly startled out of his wits.

As we follow Jesus, we find out that He is and has always been with us. The Lorica of St. Patrick, written, as tradition has it, by

St. Patrick for protection in bringing the gospel to Ireland, puts it this way:

> May Christ shield me today.
> Christ with me, Christ before me,
> Christ behind me,
> Christ in me, Christ beneath me,
> Christ above me,
> Christ on my right, Christ on my left,
> Christ when I lie down, Christ when I sit,
> Christ when I stand,
> Christ in the heart of everyone who thinks of me,
> Christ in the mouth of everyone who speaks of me,
> Christ in every eye that sees me,
> Christ in every ear that hears me.[3]

What wonderful truth. Christ within me. Christ above me. Christ in every eye that sees me and every ear that hears me. Christ when I lie down, Christ when I sit, Christ when I stand. And for a heartbroken eight-year-old girl, Christ when I wash dishes. Christ is *always* near. Christ is nearer to us than even a mom with her little ones.

As we watch our children imitate us, let it be a reminder of how we're to humbly imitate Jesus, firm in the knowledge that as we do so, Jesus is pursuing us, surrounding us with the protection of His loving care, and freeing us from any obstacles to the full and abundant life He offers.

Reflection Questions on Humble Imitation

1. Can you think of a time when you have attempted to follow God and failed? How have you dealt with that disappointment? What does the way we view our failure to imitate God say about our concept of God's character?

2. Can you recall a time in your life when you knew God was pursuing you? What did that feel like?

3. What Scriptures remind you of God's faithfulness to be with you? Deuteronomy 31:6, Psalm 37:28, Psalm 94:14, Isaiah 42:16, and Hebrews 13:5 are a few good places to start.

4. Are there painful areas of your life that God is calling you to leave behind as you follow Him? Jesus came to set you free. Pray that the Lord would open your eyes to see Him at work in your situation and to experience His forgiveness, freedom, and pursuit of you.

5. In what areas of your life is God calling you to imitate Him now? Are you experiencing His presence with you there? If not, what aspect of His character are you not believing? Ask Him to grant you faith to believe that He is who He says He is.

2

Living Beloved

*Before I shaped you in the womb, I knew all
about you. Before you saw the light of day,
I had holy plans for you: A prophet to the
nations—that's what I had in mind for you.*

—JEREMIAH 1:5, MSG

A t age thirteen months, it was his first Bible study. And he was overwhelmed. With a look of utter terror, baby Josiah was thrust into the eager arms of a mom whose children were nearly too big to snuggle close while his own mom took off her coat. With anxious looks and trembling lip, Josiah glanced in rapid succession from one face to another. "This place is not safe," his expression seemed to say.

But within moments of sitting down on the floor with his mom, a smile emerged. It wasn't long before Josiah was looking bravely around the room, engaging each woman, smiling, cooing, and laughing. Then he was standing, grasping the coffee table and showing off his toy cars. The shy, overwhelmed child had been transformed into a confident baby enjoying the spotlight. Every so often, though, Josiah would glance back, making sure his mom was still behind him. Baby Josiah could face the sea of unknown faces, enjoy them even, because his mom was right there with him. He was living beloved.

Small children show us that the crucial thing to knowing who we are is not inward introspection (though of course there is value in being self-aware) but in knowing *whose* we are. As with baby Josiah, their identity and sense of well-being is wrapped up not in themselves but in their mothers. Like a small child who glances back to find his mom, in order to discover who we are, we must look upward not inward. The key to our identity is not "I" but I Am—Yahweh, LORD, God—the one who created us and loves us, the one who is the same yesterday, today, and forever (Hebrews 13:8).

The key is living in the knowledge that God loves us individually, wholly, and unconditionally, regardless of our accomplishments, efforts, talents, or goals. Children show us how. As we study our own little ones, we see that their world revolves around us, their parents who love them unconditionally. Does our world revolve around God? Do we accept His love as our children accept ours? Children remind us that we are

- daughters,
- beloved,
- ones in whom the Lord is well pleased, and
- known.

DAUGHTERS ONE AND ALL

There are countless ways in which Jesus was different from us when He lived on earth some two thousand years ago. For starters, He lived a perfect, blameless life. He was completely without sin, wholly righteous, and unbelievably strong and gracious, willing to pay the ultimate price for strangers. Yet, another difference is key to all Jesus accomplished: Jesus knew who He was. He lived life as a chosen, beloved son. Jesus knew who He was because He knew *whose* He was.

At Jesus' baptism, the proud Father God spoke. The heavens opened and the Spirit descended as a dove and rested on Jesus. "This is my beloved Son, with whom I am well pleased," God proclaimed (Matthew 3:16-17. See Luke 3:21-22; Mark 1:9-11). This was *the* pivotal moment in Jesus' ministry. The Father God introduced Jesus to the listening world. The words He chose were life-giving and utterly transformative because they spoke deeply about Jesus' identity. God tells Jesus three essential truths about His identity. Jesus is

- a son,
- beloved,
- and one in whom His Father God is well pleased.

When we think about it, the words the Lord spoke over Jesus at His baptism are somewhat surprising. God was revealing who Jesus is, His true identity. Yet the words God used to identify Jesus do not include *Savior* or *King* or *Creator* of the world—though Jesus is surely all of these things—but *Son*. When God revealed Jesus, He broadcast their *relationship*. To be sure, the Lord was also declaring Jesus to be Lord of all, but the most important thing was that Jesus was God's Son.

The remarkable thing is that Jesus *believed His Father*. He believed to the core of His being that He was God's Son, that He was beloved, and that the Father was pleased with Him. In John 5:20, for example, He matter-of-factly states, "The Father loves the

Son." While the Pharisees, religious leaders, and even Jesus' own family doubted His identity, Jesus remained steadfast. He knew who He was.

Scripture tells us that it was out of this life-giving, fully internalized knowledge that Jesus' ministry flourished. Because He was a son, He could say, "I know where I came from and where I am going" (John 8:14). He knew He was chosen and sent. He had a place, a purpose, and a mission. Jesus was able to go to the cross boldly and defeat death once for all because He knew who He was: the Son of God come to mend a broken world.

While the work of being made in Christ's image will never be finished here on earth, *we do share fully in His identity*. Scripture reveals that we are joint heirs with Christ. Regardless of our station, position, family, or past—as believers, we are chosen and beloved daughters of the King Most High. Through Jesus, in Jesus, we have been given "the right to become [His] children" (John 1:12), children who can call God their Abba Father, or dear Daddy.

My husband told me about a colleague who was expecting a second child. He and his wife had worked hard to prepare their older daughter for a new sibling. They had answered questions about Mommy's growing tummy; awkwardly discussed where babies come from; read lots of books about being a big sister; and talked about how babies eat, cry, and stink a lot. They had even explained that, due to a C-section, Mommy would be unable to carry big sis for a couple of weeks after the baby was born. To celebrate their last night as a family of three, they went to dinner. Mom and Dad were feeling confident in their preparation and proud of themselves as parents when their daughter asked this question: "And how long will the baby be staying?"

This little girl's identity was as a beloved child of her parents—an only child. The thought that anyone else might also occupy that space with her was inconceivable. She was the beloved. She was the one in whom her parents delighted. It was incomprehensible to her that she might be asked to share all of that love, all of that delight, all of that *identity* with someone else.

Psalm 139:13-14 reminds us of the special care the Lord took with each of us—as if we, too, were His only child. His only child. "For You formed my inward parts; You wove me in my mother's womb. I will give thanks to You, for I am fearfully and wonderfully made" (NASB). The truths of this passage are worthy of a good soak. None of us is an accident. No one is a product of biology alone. The Lord of the universe is Master Creator. He's the one who skillfully wrought and delighted in all that we are; He's the one who adopts us as daughters; and He's the one who thought us worth the ultimate sacrifice. We need never hunger or thirst for love or relationship or identity or worth.

Like Jesus, we are heirs. Jesus' identity as God's child is our identity as well. We have been made righteous by the blood of Jesus. We stand in His place; we're the chosen, the sent, the beloved. And we can rejoice in this identity and say along with the disciple John, "What marvelous love the Father has extended to us! Just look at it—we're called children of God! That's who we really are" (1 John 3:1, MSG).

Dear one, hear me today. No matter what your day has looked like so far—if you've yelled at your kids as I did mine this morning—no matter your flaws and sinfulness, no matter that you sometimes find God's promises difficult to believe completely, if you've accepted Christ as your Savior you are a daughter of God. That is who you really are. He has adopted you once for all. And He loves you with a never-ending, always-and-forever love.

What might it look like to live from that realization? Let's take a close look at the Father's relationship with His Son.

You Are Beloved

When the Spirit of God descended over the waters of Jesus' baptism, God chose to reveal not only Jesus' sonship but also His pleasure. The Father introduced Jesus to the world He would save not with trumpet blast and grand parade but with a simple affirmation: Jesus was beloved and pleasing to God. That the Lord chose to reveal these two particular pieces of information demonstrates how crucial being beloved and winsome is to Jesus' identity—and to our identity.

The original Greek word used for beloved, *agapetos*, literally means "divinely loved." Jesus was divinely loved. Notice that God does not speak about Jesus' obedience or His faithfulness or His giftings or even about His God-given mission of righting every wrong, bringing salvation to a waiting world and humanity back into relationship with its Creator God. Instead, God declares that Jesus is divinely loved *because* He is the Son. No explanation needed. No qualifiers attached.

At the same time, the world learns that God the Father is well pleased with Jesus. Well pleased is translated from the original Greek word *eudokeo*, which communicates that God thinks well of His Son, approves of Him, and takes pleasure in Him. Again, God does not catalogue the traits that make Jesus pleasing to Him. Jesus is pleasing to the Lord simply because He is.

Similarly, the worth of a beloved daughter cannot be measured. It is not in what we do, accumulate, or accomplish. In fact, Jesus explained that our "work" is not work at all. After feeding the five thousand, He urged the listening crowd to work for eternal treasure not wealth, power, possessions, or prestige. "Do not labor for the food which perishes, but for the food which endures to eternal life, which the Son of Man will give to you" (John 6:27, NASB). The disciples were keenly interested. Likely thinking of their to-do list, which doubtless included many worthwhile endeavors, they questioned Him: "What must we do, to be doing the works of God?" (John 6:28). Notice the emphasis: "What must we *do?*"

You may have wondered along with the disciples what Jesus requires of you today. And you may have answered (as I often do) this question with these types of thoughts: *We should be taking care of young children, working with excellence, bringing a meal to the new mom down the street, leading a Bible study, throwing a welcome party for the new family on the cul-de-sac, being a supportive spouse, finally signing up to sponsor a child through Compassion International.* Surely, these are some of the examples of "work" that Jesus would recite.

But Jesus answered: "This is the work of God, that you believe in him whom he has sent" (John 6:29). I am flabbergasted along with the disciples. *What? You can't be serious, Lord,* I think. *There is so much to do!* Yet Jesus' quiet answer reverberates through time and into my heart: "The work of God is *to believe.*" The first thing, the only thing, God requires of me is that I believe in Him.

Jesus' answer would make perfect sense to children. Toddlers don't think of their days in terms of accomplishments. Before bed, they don't check off tasks and stew over those left unfinished. They don't recount their successful endeavors and lament those that went

less than swimmingly. At day's end, kids think in terms of relationships not tasks: Nana and Papa visited, or more recently and
uniquely, the *Easter Bunny* visited. (He really did; my mother-in-
law brought a six-foot-tall rabbit for Easter last year.) If children
stay up late, it isn't to worry about unfinished business but to snuggle with Mom and Dad or tease their brother and sister. They are
content in the simplicity of being beloved sons and daughters.

In fact, one question is nearly guaranteed to get a nonresponse
from my kiddos: "What did you do today?" No matter what the day
held—preschool, swimming lessons, a trip to the zoo—my boys
have nothing to say. No amount of asking can induce them to di-
vulge a single activity that took place that day. Occasionally, my
oldest one will offer an exasperated one-word reply: "Nothing." The
only thing worse than asking my boys what they did that day is to
ask them what they learned at school. My youngest will reply suc-
cinctly, "Not anything."

As exasperating as my children's unresponsiveness can be, I
wonder if their inattention to describing productive activity is part
of the childlikeness to which Jesus calls us. Maybe our kids have
it right when they fail to order their day around a list of activities
and accomplishments. Maybe their ability to live in the moment,
their utter unconcern with productivity, their contentment in simply enjoying those with whom they are present at the moment (not
scrolling through their Facebook feed or checking their email as I
find myself doing too often) is part of the childlikeness that Jesus
was speaking of when He gathered the little children close.

In introducing Jesus to us, the Father God affirms our deepest
need for identity. He speaks directly into who Jesus is. He speaks

directly into who we are. And as God is wont to do, He upends our world. Our identity is not reducible to our roles as mom, doctor, grandmom, editor, or coach. As important as our work and our family are to the Lord, they are *not* our identity. When we accept Christ as Savior, we stand in His place. The angels rejoice and the heavens open. Dear one, hear the Lord today as He looks down from on high and in an unmistakable, joy-filled voice says, "This is my beloved daughter in whom I am well pleased."

We need to live as Jesus did, with childlike confidence in our identity. Jesus did not question whether He was loved or why He was loved. He had no doubt that He was beloved and pleasing to the Lord: "He who sent me is with me. He has not left me alone, for I always do the things that are pleasing to him" (John 8:29). Despite the persecution, lies, and Satan's temptation; despite the religious leaders' views that He was a nobody from a nowhere town; and despite His own family's suspicion that He was crazy, Jesus stood firm in His identity. He never once doubted that He was divinely loved.

In Christ, we have an *agapetos* identity. We are divinely loved.

Living Known

Even before God the Father reveals Jesus He *sees* His Son. "*This*," God says, "is my beloved Son" (Matthew 3:16, emphasis mine). Before God gets to the powerful descriptors about who Jesus is, before God confirms Jesus' identity as Son, God notices Him. God sees Jesus. God sees Him and identifies Him in all of His uniqueness.

And God *sees* you. One of my favorite Old Testament names for God is El Roi—the God who sees me. We have an identity because God sees us and knows us.

I'm reminded of the first time I held each of my two boys. After their births, the boys were each immediately whisked away to waiting doctors' arms. There was no opportunity to see them, to hold them, to love them. This anxious mama waited an interminable amount of time, until red faced and diaper clad, they were placed in my arms. It was only then that I could finally say, "This is my son." With this simple phrase, my heart was saying so much:

I see you, little one.

I am delighted with you.

I cannot wait to get to know you, to see you grow.

You have unique callings and giftings.

I love you more than life itself.

Our desire to be known is powerful; this desire was woven into the very fabric of our being. It has been said that the greatest yearning—and greatest fear—we have as humans is to be known. We long to be accepted as we truly are. We long to have our greatest triumphs, our unique giftings, our quirky personalities, and our deepest dreams uncovered and lovingly examined. And with trembling, we long to have our worst failures laid bare—to have our anxieties, fears, and wayward thoughts revealed—and despite all of our flaws, to be wholly and unconditionally loved.

This longing is met in relationship with God the Father, who *knows* us precisely in the way we desire. The Scriptures tell us that the Lord sees everything; nothing is hidden from Him (Hebrews 4:13). What is more, the Holy Spirit searches us and knows us far better than we know ourselves. He knows every mistake we've made, even the sins of which we are unaware. God knows when we sit and when we stand. He understands our thoughts, knows our words before we say them, and is acquainted with all of our ways. He knows what makes us laugh and what makes us cry. He knows the deepest desires of our hearts. God knows *everything* about us— and He still sent His only Son to die for us!

Only God can meet our intense longing to be known and accepted. His complete intimacy and unconditional love are part of our inheritance as believers. In John 10:14, Jesus calls Himself the Good Shepherd who knows each and every one of His sheep. He knows them by their voices, their mannerisms, their personalities, their joys, their sorrows, perhaps even by their smells! Jesus knows us fully, individually, and uniquely. Not only that, but on the eve of His execution, Jesus prayed for His disciples in what is known as the High Priestly Prayer. The prayer begins with this truth: "And this is eternal life, that they *know* you, the only true God, and Jesus Christ whom you have sent" (John 17:3, emphasis mine). What a powerful truth: The very definition of eternal life includes *knowing* and *being known by* God.

And there's more. As Jeremiah 1:5 tells us, "Before you saw the light of day, I had holy plans for you" (MSG). You were created with a special purpose in mind, a holy plan set aside just for you. The Lord's words are as much for us today as they were for Jeremiah centuries ago. Before the Lord formed you, He knew you. He consecrated you, and He commissioned you for holy purposes.

One day, as we were driving along, my oldest son showed me the joy of being known. He was in his own world, buckled up in his car seat, singing softly: "Go, Elijah, go; zooming up to Bortron 7." I was delighted by his modification of the theme song from his favorite show, *Go, Diego, Go!*, and by the playful entry of Bortron 7, the home planet of the protagonist in another favorite show, *Ready Jet Go*. (Notice the common theme of *going*.) Elijah looked up to see me watching him. As awareness set in, his shy smile turned broad. His face lit up and he began to sing more loudly. Elijah knew I was delighted with his song but understood that I was even more delighted with him. He was seen and known.

Jesus sees you right where you are today. Right now. He sees you in your joy. He sees you in your pain. He knows about your frustrations and your disappointments, and He shares in them with you. He knows your dreams and your desires. He delights in your unique design. Jesus *knows you*, dear one. And He loves you.

In a parenting class at our church, the instructor urged us moms to facilitate in our children a strong sense of self. We were created in the image of God, he explained, and one of God's attributes is a strong sense of identity. When Moses asks God to identify Himself, for example, God does not hesitate but boldly proclaims, "I Am Who I Am *and* What I Am, *and* I Will Be What I Will Be" (Exodus 3:14, AMPC).

Jesus, too, had a steadfast self-image. He frequently spoke about His identity: "I am the vine; you are the branches. . . . Apart from me you can do nothing" (John 15:5). "I am the way, and the truth, and the life" (John 14:6). As His image bearers, we reflect that strong sense of secure identity—an identity born not of accomplishments but of a deep realization of who we are in the Lord.

We can be strong and steadfast because we have a risen Lord who adores us. Our identity and our fate are secure. For our every doubt, He answers I Am. I Am with you. I Am the God who sustains you and upholds the work of your hands. I Am the God who will never forsake you nor forget you. I Am the God who guides you, who rescues you, and who delights in you. I Am the God who became flesh and died on a cross so you might spend eternity with me. I. Am.

"We are all worms," Winston Churchill famously said. "But I do believe that I am a glow-worm."[1] It's hard for me to imagine this sort of self-confidence. But Churchill was right. The truth is that God's grace makes us all glow. He chose us, even when we were the least. He created us, designed us, reached down from on high and rescued us, and loves us unconditionally. He chose us when we were weak, fallen, and overlooked. And He makes us radiant. We are fallen sinners, worms one and all, but we glow in the light of His grace.

My boys love an event, and my sister's wedding was no exception. Our family had just been through a statewide campaign as my husband ran to serve as Missouri's attorney general. We attended campaign events as a family as much as possible, so the boys met countless people, listened to countless speeches, and ate lots of chicken. Elijah was just old enough to catch a bit of the goings-on. His favorite part of the events came when his dad's speeches concluded; there was often applause and the opportunity to meet people and shake their hands. Elijah basked in all the clapping and became an expert handshaker.

When my sister got married later that year, Elijah and Blaise were darling ring bearers (says their unbiased mom), but once they began literally to kick off their boots during the ceremony, they were removed to safer terrain. At the end of the ceremony, the groom kissed the bride and everyone clapped. Elijah perked up, assuming the applause was for him. Then he turned to his dad and remarked with all sincerity, "They will all want to shake my hand." Indeed.

Dear sister, as you go about your day today or start the day fresh tomorrow, study your children. Observe them as they live within the knowledge that they are beloved and pleasing to you, their mom, regardless of what they accomplish or fail to accomplish. Let their ability to live beloved speak to and encourage you. Dear one, the Lord longs for you to live in freedom as a dearly beloved daughter. When He sees you, He sees someone who glows. Hear Him today, right now, as He says with authority, power, and joy, "This is my beloved daughter in whom I am well pleased."

Reflection Questions on Living Beloved

1. How do you view yourself? Are you a mom, teacher, pianist, runner? Who does God say you are? For a reminder, read Romans 8:15, John 1:12, and Jeremiah 1:5.

2. Do you believe you are first and foremost a beloved daughter, perfectly pleasing to the Father God who knows you and created you with a specific purpose in mind? Why or why not?

3. Is there a time when you can remember feeling beloved just because you were you?

4. How would your life change if you internalized your identity as a beloved and pleasing daughter of God?

3
Living All-In

*Have I not commanded you? Be strong
and courageous. Do not be frightened,
and do not be dismayed, for the LORD your
God is with you wherever you go.*

—JOSHUA 1:9

My friend looked blankly across the table at me, seemingly puzzled as I said, "I'm afraid they get that from me." We were discussing our toddlers, who are great friends and polar opposites. Sarah's boy is a cautious, dark-headed, gentle giant. Elijah and Blaise are pint-sized towheads with a penchant for mischief. They live life with a verve that is both heartwarming and terrifying. (Sarah, a psychology professor, says my children cause her cortisol levels to rise to dangerous levels.) Yet my friend saw none of that boldness in me (or maybe I'm the one who no longer saw such boldness in myself).

She didn't know that I used to be that child—the one who wouldn't take no for an answer. As my friend and I sipped coffee that morning, memories of my skinny six-year-old self returned. It was morning recess at school, and the monkey bars beckoned. As

I reached my scrawny arms up to grab a bar, I heard an older voice say, "You're too little. If you try, you'll fall and break your arm." The gauntlet had been thrown.

I'm sure that, even then, pride was a motivating factor in my decision to ignore that warning. But there also was boldness, courage, the willingness to risk. Though the monkey bars did prove too much for me that day—yes, I *did* fall and break my arm—I nevertheless long for that childlike readiness to step out in faith, to be bold and courageous, to live all-in.

As my heart rejoices in my boys' courageous and adventuresome spirits, it also aches with longing. What happened to my own sense of adventure? What happened to the courageous girl who would be the first to enter a public-speaking contest, the first in her family to attend graduate school? When did I become timid? When did the world's challenges, and its opportunities, become too risky? When did a move to another state, leaving dear friends and a church family, become so scary? The real question underlying all of these others is this: When did God (or, more accurately, my perception of Him) become any less God?

It's no surprise that I want to recapture that childlike sense of adventure. The Bible tells us that we were created for and called forth to live an all-in life. We are Christ's workmanship, created for the good works God has prepared, equipped, and empowered us to do (Ephesians 2:10). He has given us a spirit, not of fear, but of power and might and a sound mind (2 Timothy 1:7).

The idea of living boldly is nothing new. Time and again, the Israelites were urged to live all-in. In Joshua 1, for example, God issues a surprising edict to the Israelites' new leader, Joshua. Joshua is to lead the Israelites into the Promised Land. In this mission, the Lord promises to grant Joshua success and demands that he be courageous. In the space of just a few verses, God presses this command upon Joshua *three* times.

There's no question: God envisions bold lives for us as believers. That's easier said than done, we protest. Life is difficult, and fear is real. Our daily lives can be consumed with health issues, heart issues, and the pain of broken relationships. We might have to move far from home and leave behind family and friends. We know the pain of feeling overlooked by our spouses; we know the agony of waiting for motherhood; and we know the difficulty of bearing children into a sin-wrecked world for which we are insufficient to prepare them. It's a challenge to live boldly, courageously. But chances are, given the Lord's repeated encouragement, Joshua didn't feel like a superhero either. We're in good company.

Many of the heroes of the Bible were reluctant ones. They had to be coaxed into fulfilling the Lord's grand plan for them. Moses refused to go unless Aaron went to speak for him. Jeremiah protested that he was only a boy. Gideon asked for a sign—and then another one. And Joshua needed constant reassurance.

God's unceasing encouragement of Joshua is evidence that He knows how overwhelmed we can feel. But it's in the fear and brokenness that He operates. After all, Jesus came to earth to bring the Good News to the hurting and afflicted, to bind up the brokenhearted, and to proclaim liberty and freedom to those held captive by fear (Isaiah 61:1).

As my two brave boys make my own cortisol levels rise, I feel them steadfastly pulling me back into the land of courageousness.

They live all-in. And through them, God is graciously showing me how to live all-in. Children live courageously because they

- know they are not in control;
- are rooted and grounded in love;
- and are unafraid to dream the impossible.

NOT IN CONTROL

I watch as my two-year-old scampers up the obstacle course. Foot after foot, knee after knee, hand over hand, until suddenly down he goes. I rush to catch him, and my heart beats wildly at the near fall. Blaise is completely impervious to his narrowly missed head injury and breaks into a wide grin. No fear, this one. He often has absolute confidence in his ability to do *anything* that his older brother can do—so long as Mom is not far behind. And the truth hits me: My son can live courageously because he knows I will catch him. My son can live all-in because he knows he isn't in control.

Courage is the stuff of childhood because children know someone else is at the helm. Children—from the reckless to the more cautious—are free to enjoy every moment of childhood because they know that the big details of life are entrusted to their parents. Like the birds of Matthew's parable (Matthew 6:26), well-loved children have no reason to worry about food, clothing, shelter, or safety. Children can live all-in because they *are dependent.*

While children sometimes chafe under their parents' authority, it is also enormously freeing for them. A sociological study revealed that children play more boldly at recess if the playground is enclosed. When the fence line was clearly visible during the study, the children played confidently, roaming to the farthest reaches of the property. Conversely, when there was no fence or boundary, the children stayed close and played fearfully. Without the protection of the fence, the children were less free.[1]

That truth is worth sitting with. We can live boldly and courageously, we can live all-in, because someone else is at the helm. As much as we think we would like to be, we simply are not in control. Dear one, this is a *good* thing, because the God who loves you and created the entire universe is the one in charge.

It's been said that, with the fateful choice to eat of the fruit of the tree of knowledge of good and evil, Adam and Eve traded in relationship for the *appearance* of control. That is, they wanted to *know* the difference between good and evil. Rather than resting in the Father's provision of everything good in the Garden of Eden, they chose independence and self-sufficiency. Some Bible scholars think that the author of Genesis was using a literary device called a merism when he wrote the Hebrew phrase for good and evil, עָרָו בוֹט. A merism pairs opposite terms together to create a broader meaning; so the contrasting phrase *good and evil* would mean "everything." Thus, Adam and Eve chose to eat of the fruit of the tree of knowledge in order to know "everything."

Regardless of whether the writer of Genesis intended the specific or the broader meaning, we know that Adam and Eve ate because they desired knowledge, or control. In a way, Adam and Eve grew up when they ate of the forbidden fruit. They traded in childlike dependence, security, and relationship to grasp at self-direction and self-control.

We can see their choice reverberating through the ages as we desperately try to control our own situations, our own direction, our own lives, and our own children. On a daily basis, we trade in relationship and dependency on God for the appearance of control. We trust in other people or in our own knowledge, efforts, and wisdom. Because we're calling the shots, we're often fearful of making mistakes and getting it wrong. And in all of our striving, we forget what it means to rest in the One who is faithful. We forget how to live boldly as children of God, knowing He is always on our side, constantly looking out for us.

But the amazing thing is that God issues us an open invitation to come back into relationship with Him, to lay our life at His feet. He offers to exchange our burdens for His easy yoke. No strings attached.

Dear sister, if you haven't yet accepted Jesus' invitation to come to Him, now is the perfect time. Jesus wants to call you His own and is waiting for you with open arms. He wants you to live in freedom here on earth and to give you the gift of eternal life with Him in heaven. All Jesus asks is that you repent of your sin, acknowledge your deep need for Him, and believe that He died on a cross and rose again in order to save you. As Romans 10:9 explains, "If you confess with your mouth that Jesus is Lord and believe in your heart that God raised him from the dead, you will be saved."

If you've never given your heart to Jesus, this simple prayer by Dr. Ray Pritchard shows you how.

Lord Jesus, for too long I've kept you out of my life. I
know that I am a sinner and that I cannot save myself.
No longer will I close the door when I hear you knocking.
By faith I gratefully receive your gift of salvation. I am
ready to trust you as my Lord and Savior. Thank you, Lord
Jesus, for coming to earth. I believe you are the Son of

God who died on the cross for my sins and rose from the dead on the third day. Thank you for bearing my sins and giving me the gift of eternal life. I believe your words are true. Come into my heart, Lord Jesus, and be my Savior. Amen.[2]

Children teach us how to accept all that Jesus came to give us. They teach us how to be comfortable with dependency. Ironically, knowing that we aren't in control allows us to live boldly, wildly, and freely in the love of the Lord. It is only in His arms that we are able to be all that He created us to be.

Rooted and Grounded in Love

Despite being barely two years old, Blaise views himself as a force to be reckoned with. No one is better at parting a crowd. He gives no berth and takes no prisoners.

The place he loves best in the whole wide world is lovingly known as "the bounce place." The Tiger Bounce entertainment center is the mecca of all meccas for the moms of young boys, offering enormous bounce houses, slides, trampolines, and Legos. (For those truly desperate moms among us, they offer a monthly family pass for twenty-five dollars. Best money spent all winter.) The place promises loads of fun with a bonus: guaranteed afternoon naps and restored souls for moms.

My two youngsters have become somewhat notorious at the bounce place. On one particularly crowded day, Blaise, not yet two, was scaling the most difficult slide using a series of steps and ropes. He was moving from foothold to foothold as fast as his short legs would allow. Two older girls, probably four and five, were behind him. Impatient, they crowded him, urging him on. Finally, he'd had enough. Without missing a beat, he backed them off with a well-placed hiney-check. You've never seen a better box out. Without a backward glance, Blaise continued on his mission.

And this was not the only time that Blaise has set someone straight. "Is it time to go pick up your brother from preschool, Elijah?" I ask.

A look of complete and utter disbelief meets my eyes in the rearview mirror. It takes him a few beats, and then my two-year-old carefully enunciates, as if *he* were the adult talking to a small child, "*I'm* not Elijah. *I'm* Blaisie."

This, unfortunately, is not the only time I've called him by his older brother's name and vice versa. I'm sure it won't be the last. But I love Blaise's sense of self.

In a way unique to a two-year-old who has yet to realize his limits, Blaise goes through life without doubts. He occupies fully the space he has been given. He takes possession of it, seeing, touching, tasting, and living. Children live all-in because they are rooted and grounded in love. Their faith is in someone bigger than themselves.

Hebrews 11 is the Bible's Hall of Faith. It's startlingly refreshing because the heroes were very normal. Like us, they were deeply flawed; they sinned and fell short. Like us, they doubted. Many of them were reluctant heroes who did not at first accept God's call. These less-than-enthusiastic heroes of the faith ultimately were able to live all-in because they knew who was in their corner. Throughout the span of the Old Testament, in stories recounted by different authors in different eras about incredibly different men and women, the key to living out God's call was always the same: a childlike realization that the Lord was with them, that He was there to catch them should they fall.

Through a burning bush, God memorably called Moses forth to rescue the Israelites from Egyptian oppression. Moses was aghast. He was somebody turned nobody. He had traded in royal position for sheep tending in the backwaters of a desert wilderness. He had committed murder and fled from Egypt in disgrace. Like so many of our champions of the faith, Moses was not an obvious hero. Moses thus protested: "*Who am I* that I should go to Pharaoh and bring the children of Israel out of Egypt?" (Exodus 3:11, emphasis mine). The Lord answered simply: "But I will be with you" (Exodus 3:12).

The Lord's call to Gideon was strikingly similar. Gideon was *hiding* from the Midianites when an angel of the Lord appeared and said, "The LORD is with you, O mighty man of valor" (Judges 6:12). The Lord then commanded Gideon: "Go in this might of yours and save Israel from the hand of Midian" (Judges 6:14). The hidden Gideon was incredulous. He was a wholly unsuitable hero. Not only was his clan the weakest in all of Israel, but he was the least in his father's house. In an answer stretching across time and circumstances, the Lord gave Gideon precisely the same response He gave Moses: "But I will be with you" (Judges 6:16).

Jeremiah's hang-up was his youth. When the Lord called him to speak truth to a wayward Israel, he said no. "Ah, Lord GOD! Behold, I do not know how to speak, for I am only a youth" (Jeremiah 1:6). The Lord brooked no excuse. He commanded Jeremiah to go to whom he was sent and to speak the words he was given. He had nothing to fear because I Am was going to be with him. Jeremiah's weaknesses mattered not *"for I am with you* to deliver you" (Jeremiah 1:8, emphasis mine).

We also have a catalogue of excuses that we pull out when the Lord calls us to walk boldly. And they seem so *legitimate.* Can't God see that we're simply insufficient for the task? For me right now, insufficiency reverberates through the call of motherhood. I often feel exhausted and ill-equipped, all poured out. Who am I to speak life into young souls and to discipline with consistency when I'm the one who so often falls short? Who am I to love with a love that is supposed to model the Father's love, for heaven's sake? Who am I to raise up these two young boys to know and love the Lord? Some days it's all I can do to keep them *safe.*

So often when we are called, we focus on ourselves. *"Who am I*, Lord?" we ask. But the Lord always answers a different question. When we—along with Moses, Gideon, and Jeremiah—ask "Who am I, Lord?" God shifts the focus from ourselves to Himself. He doesn't reassure us with a list of our past accomplishments or even remind us of the talents and gifts He has given to us. Rather, the answer to any doubt—youth, circumstances, experience, past sin, weakness, and exhaustion—is always the same: *"But I will be with you."*

End of story. When the Lord calls us to be part of His plan, to be His hands and feet here on earth, He calls us into a childlike relationship of dependency. He knows we're insufficient. But that's beside the point. The Lord answers *all* with six simple words: "But I will be with you." No matter our circumstances, giftings, or perceived lack of giftings, the Lord brings us to places where we can fulfill the calls He has on our lives by virtue of His presence and power. He is with us.

Our reluctant spiritual giants were able to live boldly because their hearts trusted in the presence of the Lord. Ironically, these heroes of the faith had to become like little children to go about their God-given tasks. It takes a childlike comfort with dependency to know that the Lord's presence is all that is required.

In short, the key to courageous living (as to everything) is Jesus. Jesus promises that He will be with us all of our days and that He will never leave us or forsake us. Our childlike task is to be rooted and grounded in that love. To find our identities in Jesus. To lean into His presence. To listen as the Lord quiets our hearts and speaks love into them: "Do not be frightened, and do not be dismayed, for the LORD your God is with you wherever you go" (Joshua 1:9).

As Deuteronomy explains, God has given us our places on earth. We are right where we're supposed to be, vested with special calls on our lives. We are to "go up, take possession" (Deuteronomy 1:21), and we need not be afraid or discouraged, because the Lord our God is with us. He goes before us and is with us; there is no place beyond His presence. He keeps us wherever we go and brings us back to Himself. He strengthens us and helps us. He upholds us with His right hand. Because the Lord is our light and our salvation, we have nothing to fear. Nothing can thwart His plans; He will accomplish His good work in us and through us.

Blaise's two-year-old bravado, his sense of place, even his well-placed hiney-checks, are based on dependence. Blaise can boldly conquer imaginary worlds and the very real kingdom he knows as the bounce place because he knows that his mom is right there with him.

In the chaos of motherhood, hear the Lord's gentle whisper to me and to you. "Fear not, O mighty woman of valor. I am with you.

I am with you in the middle-of-the-night feedings, and I am with you during the long daytime hours. I am with you when discipline is a struggle and when you don't know what to do. I am with you when you are flat-out exhausted. I am with you when your patience has been tested—and when it has broken. I am with you during each new season of motherhood." Precious mama, hear the Lord today: "I am with you, O mighty woman of valor. Go in this might of yours and pursue the work I've given you with abandon."

DREAMING BIG

Children have the most interesting dreams. Blaise loves food. And he frequently dreams about its absence. The other evening, he awoke from a nightmare, exclaiming, "Maaammmaaa, he (presumably older brother) ate all of my Goldfish crackers." The following night, after a day that included the trauma of being told he could *not* eat his playdate's yogurt, he woke up hollering, "I wwwaaannnttt yogurt." The plaintive cry of the truly bereft.

Aside from food dreams, many of our children's dreams inspire.

"Mama, this car can fly."

"Mama, I'm going to be a police officer when I grow up."

"Mama, I'm going to stay with you always."

A child's world is one dream, one possibility, after another.

As women, as moms, it's easy to become so immersed in the day-to-day that we forget to dream, or maybe we forget *how* to dream. Eugene Peterson all too casually points out a paradox about the human condition: "The puzzle is why so many people live so badly. Not so wickedly, but so inanely."[3]

The word *inanely* jumps from the page. Do I live my very full life inanely? Surely. At times. Sometimes we believe the lie that life is to be trudged through until we meet Jesus face-to-face. Not that the promise of eternal life is not grand enough. It is. Not that every difficult moment will become insignificant in His light. It will. But a trudging sort of existence fails to believe the Lord's grand promises for life here and now. It forgets that we are in Christ Jesus and that He is present within us this very instant. It forgets that He calls us to live wholly and completely *right now*.

When God is our Father, the sky *really* is the limit. As our children imagine careers as doctors, police officers, astronauts, and cowboys, they show us how to dream. Indeed, when Jesus speaks of the Kingdom of Heaven being made up of children He's likely thinking of, among other things, their exuberant embrace of the impossible. Children are not yet conditioned to dream only reasonable, readily attainable dreams. They dare to dream the impossible.

And of course, the impossible is precisely what God makes possible. As Jesus said in Mark 10:27, "All things are possible with God." Over and over, the Bible reminds us that nothing is too difficult for the Lord. It strikes me as a grace that many of these Old Testament miracles have to do with motherhood: Sarah conceived when she was too old, Mary when she was a virgin, and Elizabeth though she was barren. For the God who created the stars and calls them forth, nothing is impossible.

Even more, when kids dream they are living out God's image in them—the created image of a God who dreams big. God, after all, was hardly thinking small when He created the majestic universe. And He created children, and us, with an immense capacity for dreams.

The remedy to living inanely, Eugene Peterson writes, is to

recognize and live out God's individual call on our lives. It's to treasure His call to raise these little ones, to go about the important tasks of motherhood with purpose and design, to value our work as moms, and to offer each moment of our (often tiring) days to the Lord of lords. The way to dream big is to know deep in our bones—just like our children and our heroes of the faith—that we are called, chosen, and set apart. We can have faith with Job, despite all of our inadequacies and even in the midst of the tiredness of early mom-years, because we can dream, because we know that God "can do all things" (Job 42:2).

Children are unafraid to *live* their dreams in part because they are innately curious. They enter into their world and they interact with it. They question. They hold, taste, feel, and examine. (And who wouldn't want to see what the play rails at Burger King taste like?) They try. They dive into life with an explorer's mind-set. They make mistakes. And they don't worry about what they don't know.

Children dream large because they aren't afraid to be wrong. My boys make all sorts of absurd pronouncements every single day. The sun is a planet. There's a snake over there. Ice cream is for breakfast. It's *not* cold outside—never you mind the sleeting rain. Occasionally they are right; most often they are wrong. But this never stops them from trying again.

Our pride and desire to have it all together can keep us from laying hold of God. It can prevent us from living all-in like a child. It can stop us from praying out loud for our hurting friend or leading a Bible study. It can stop us from asking questions.

Consider the Pharisees, the religious leaders of Jesus' day who had unparalleled access to the King of kings. They repeatedly plied Jesus with loaded questions, mostly trying to trip Him up. Jesus answered with great skill and wisdom, often leaving the Pharisees looking worse for the exchange.

In Luke 20, after Jesus parried another loaded question, Luke said that the Pharisees withdrew: "For they no longer dared to ask him any question" (Luke 20:40). They had asked questions out of pride. And they stopped asking questions of Jesus because they didn't want to appear foolish.

How different are the questions of children. Children show us how to live courageously—asking, seeking, experimenting, proclaiming—because they see no need to save face. They are comfortable being wrong. They live life with the kind of energy for which I long. They dream. They take hold of the world in which we live and ask questions. Their bold lives show me what it means to live all-in. And as I watch my boys conquer unseen worlds, I feel the Lord's smile of pleasure, and I hear His whisper: "Go in this might of yours, O mighty woman of valor, for I am with you always." Dear friend, can you hear it too?

Reflection Questions on Living All-In

1. Are there areas of your life where you wish you could go "all-in" or where you are living inanely? What fears or struggles prevent you from embracing God's call to be all-in, trusting that He is in control?

2. Name a particular way that you struggle to believe in God's authority. If you are honest with yourself, where would you prefer to be in control? Write it down, or say it out loud, and confess it to God in prayer.

3. The Bible tells us that nothing is impossible with God. He is the author and perfecter of our faith and our dreams. Can you ask Him to give you a dream that is so big you cannot accomplish it without Him? Can you ask God to show you a God-sized vision for your family, your children, and your home? Do you dare to live all-in and ask for a God-sized vision for your ministry and work?

4. Are there curiosities or dreams that you have not let breathe because of fear, control, or wounds from your past? Can you see yourself as a child asking God to take your hand as you explore?

4

Transparency

*But all things become visible when they
are exposed by the light, for everything
that becomes visible is light.*

—Ephesians 5:13, nasb

"I want to go outside, *now!*" my two-year-old screamed one morning. He'd been told that we needed to have breakfast *before* watering the flowers. This did not suit. I am sure you can picture the ensuing scene. Wails, screams, fists on the floor, and then as I picked him up for a time-out, teeth! Blaise is nothing if not authentic. He had no trouble communicating his desire to go outside or expressing his displeasure. Blaise was hiding nothing. He was bracingly honest, with his very real emotions on full display.

It is not unusual for toddlers to be overwhelmed by joy, overcome with sadness, and uncontrollably angry—often all in the same breath. Small children experience incredible highs and devastating lows, and—this is key—they share those joys and disappointments with everyone in earshot. They are refreshingly transparent, especially with their parents, with whom they share every emotion.

As we grow up, we tend to leave this sort of authenticity behind. We may experience the pain of rejection and become guarded as a result. To avoid being hurt, we sometimes abandon childlike vulnerability and transparency and rely more on ourselves. We often learn to quiet our emotions, to share less, even with those to whom we are closest, even with God.

The surprising thing is not that toddlers are transparent but that this is *biblical*. When Jesus called the little children to Himself and urged His disciples to be like them, transparency was a kingdom trait that likely came to mind. Children show us that relationships blossom when we acknowledge our mistakes and insufficiencies. They teach us that real relationship depends upon authenticity— and that God not only wants to hear from us but can handle our rawest emotions.

Transparent Failures

In order to accommodate his wheelchair, our neighbor Fred built a spectacular walking path around his pond. The path is adorned with gorgeous trees, grasses, and flowering plants. Its edge shimmers reflectively as glass globes bounce back the summer sunshine and evening landscape lights. Fred and his family generously allow our boys to enjoy this oasis. We love meandering along the path and catching frogs, minnows, and tadpoles in the pond.

One day, the globes proved to be too much of a temptation for Blaise. Before I could react, he picked one up and threw it as hard as he could. The globe cracked in two.

"Oh, no," I said, "we need to find Fred and tell him we've broken his globe."

Well, find Fred we did. From behind the shelter of my legs, Blaise haltingly told Fred about breaking the globe, and that he was "sowwy."

Fred's response could not have been more generous. "It's okay, little fellow, I've broken several myself," he replied. Fred's response in the next few weeks was a picture of grace. He came out to visit with the boys more often as they played around the pond, once remarking, "I sure was proud of the little fellow's apology the other day." A week or two later, he invited the boys into his shop to see a swing he'd purchased to hang on the trees near his pond. Fred's boys are all grown, but he'd seen the swing and thought our boys might enjoy it. Blaise's confession actually brought him into closer fellowship with Fred.

The same is true for us. When we ask the Lord for forgiveness, grace flows down and we are drawn closer in fellowship with God. As 1 John 1:9 puts it, "If we confess our sins, he is faithful and just to forgive us our sins and to cleanse us from all unrighteousness." The Lord already knows our deepest regrets, but when we transparently offer them to Jesus, we become like little children crawling back up onto their parents' laps.

In fact, the very concept of repentance encompasses not just a turning away from sin but a turning *toward God*. "Repent (change your mind and purpose)," Paul urges, "turn around *and* return [to God]" (Acts 3:19, AMPC). When we repent and turn toward God, our sins are "erased" and "times of refreshing . . . come from the presence of the Lord" (Acts 3:19, AMPC).

Confession brings light and life where there was darkness and decay. King David speaks eloquently about the God-effected transition from the darkness of sin to the light of forgiveness:

For when I kept silent, my bones wasted away through my groaning all day long . . . I acknowledged my sin to you, and I did not cover my iniquity; I said, "I will confess my transgressions to the LORD," and you forgave the iniquity of my sin. (Psalm 32:3, 5)

Scripture tells us that the Lord can redeem even our worst moments. In Ephesians, Paul writes, "When anything is exposed by the light, it becomes visible, for anything that becomes visible is light" (Ephesians 5:13-14). This is the hope we have in Jesus. God can use our most regrettable mistakes when we bring them to the light of His grace. He is the God who redeems. He is the God who rebuilds broken walls and restores the years the locusts have eaten. He is the God who stands waiting with fatted calf for the first sign of His returning prodigal daughter. He is the God who casts our sins as far as the east is from the west—and remembers them no more.

His is in the business of redemption. His is not a narrow, grudging forgiveness but a broad, expansive, once-for-all forgiveness. He is the God who directed the whole course of human history toward one single purpose: your redemption and restoration. He loves you as you are, dear one, and when He looks at you He doesn't see brokenness; He sees Jesus' righteousness.

Just as Blaise's confession brought him closer to our neighbor Fred, our confession brings us into a closer relationship with God.

TRANSPARENT NEED

Elijah was in his element. We were all gathered around the dining table as he regaled Nana and Papa with the story of Moana. With wide eyes and large hand motions he told us all about her daring adventures. He'd loved seeing the movie and relished his captive audience. Of course, Blaise was not to be outdone. When Elijah finished, he jumped in with his own story about a cartoon in which a chicken ran very, very fast. His two-year-old tongue, however, refused to keep up with his thoughts. His breath came in short, quick gasps as he repeatedly tripped over his words. With utter dejection, he looked up at me, and said, "Mama, I can't say it." And he quit talking.

And the world stopped for this mama. When you are a younger sibling, you're faced with your own limitations early and often. Blaise likes nothing better than to keep up with his older brother— except when he can't. Though he will try anything his brother does, he is sometimes forced to confide in me his weaknesses: "Mama, I can't scooter as fast as Elijah" or "Mama, I can't run as fast as Elijah." As a mom, my heart breaks when I see perceived failure on my son's face.

In this instance, I drew him close. "Of course you can say it," I reassured Blaise. And with this encouragement, Blaise began again, and the whole table turned to listen to his story.

Children do not hesitate to make their needs known. As we grow up, it can become more difficult to let others in, to admit our insufficiencies, and to ask for help. But in a parent's response to a child's inadequacy, in a mom's reaching down to kiss a skinned knee, to reassure her child, to help him back up on his bike, we see that it's weakness that opens us to the Lord's presence. Our failures can be the very means God uses to draw us close and to assure us of His unconditional love.

In fact, it's only when we are weak that the cross of Christ can be our strength. Paul, a tentmaker by trade, wrote about Jesus pitching a tent over him and dwelling upon him in his weakness (as translated in the *Amplified Bible*). Paul began by asking the Lord to remove his weakness, his thorn in the flesh. The Lord responded, "My grace (My favor and loving-kindness and mercy) is enough for you . . . for *My* strength *and* power are made perfect (fulfilled and completed) *and show themselves most effective* in [your] weakness" (2 Corinthians 12:9, AMPC). Paul ended by recognizing the Lord's presence in the midst of weakness: "When I am weak [in human strength], then am I [truly] strong (able, powerful in divine strength)" (2 Corinthians 12:10, AMPC).

Paul determined to "gladly glory" (2 Corinthians 12:9, AMPC) in this weakness, not because he was a masochist, but because he knew himself to be at his best when he was weak; it was then that the strength and power of Jesus rested upon him. Paul experienced firsthand the upside-down nature of God's Kingdom: It's when we're weak, when we're insufficient and unable, that we're *truly* able. It's when we aren't enough that we're *truly* enough—through God's empowering strength. His grace is always sufficient.

We can try our level best to keep everything under control, but the reality is that we need Jesus. This is good news because Jesus came to save the lost. When He lived on earth, Jesus did not hang out with the people who had it together but with tax collectors, prostitutes, and sinners, those the world looked down upon. The religious leaders were appalled and thought Jesus' indiscriminate taste a black mark. But Jesus saw right through their self-sufficiency, saying, "It is not those who are healthy who need a physician, but those who are sick; I did not come to call the righteous, but sinners"

(Mark 2:17, NASB). Jesus, in other words, is not put off by your need for Him, but rather came to earth in order to meet you in your need. Dear one, it is okay to need Jesus. He already knows your struggles, and stands ready to pitch His tent over you and to dwell upon you.

AUTHENTIC LAMENT

It's not often that one wonders what a two-year-old is feeling; a child of this age makes an art of transparency. I think of my friend who loves to cook. She once made blue cheese mac-n-cheese for her kiddos. As her toddler picked at the new delicacy, pushing his fork around his plate, he made no effort to hide his anguished expression. No one doubted how he felt about blue cheese macaroni.

We know that authentic relationships with people require authentic communication. So why are some of us reluctant to give voice to our concerns, questions, and doubts when we are talking to and about God? As John Swinton writes in *Raging with Compassion: Pastoral Responses to the Problem of Evil*, we may incorrectly assume that "faith should not embrace negativity."[1] We may worry that "to acknowledge the reality of pain and sadness somehow diminishes God and threatens God's control over things."[2] In our attempts to protect God, or our ideas of who He should be, however, we exclude Him from our deepest struggles. When we're silent, we allow suffering to separate us from God instead of inviting Him in.

This timidity with God is something new. The Israelites saw no need to protect their God—the God who had rained down fire on false prophets, parted the Red Sea, and brought waters roaring down on Egyptian chariots. As a matter of fact, the Israelites were notoriously a *complaining* people.

Old Testament scholar Walter Brueggemann explains that the Israelites not only thought it was legitimate to complain but "developed an entire genre for lament."[3] He argues that Israel's psalms of lament, their cries of pain and confusion, and their acknowledgement of suffering, far from being the acts of a faithless people, were instead "bold act[s] of faith."[4] Brueggemann writes:

> The use of the "psalms of darkness" may be judged by the world to be acts of unfaith and failure, but for the trusting community, their use is an act of bold faith, albeit a transformed faith.
>
> It is an act of bold faith on the one hand, because it insists that the world must be experienced as it really is and not in some pretended way. On the other hand, it is bold because it insists that all such experiences of disorder are a proper subject for discourse with God.
>
> There is nothing out of bounds, nothing precluded or inappropriate. Everything properly belongs in this conversation of the heart. To withhold parts of life from that conversation is in fact to withhold parts of life from the sovereignty of God. Thus these psalms make the important connection: everything must be brought to speech, and everything brought to speech must be addressed to God, who is the final reference for all of life.[5]

Authentic communication with God is a bold act of faithfulness because it acknowledges the reality of suffering. Lament acknowledges the harsh realities of living broken in a broken world. It does not try to hide the pain with an extra layer of makeup, busyness, or distraction, but instead refuses to excise hardship from daily living. Job, for example, a man commended for his fire-tested faith, offers us an honest account of suffering. Even while professing faith, Job blames God for causing his pain and cries out, "How long will you not look away from me, nor leave me alone . . . ?" (Job 7:19). Yet lament is hopeful precisely because it refuses to be silent or acquiescent. It refuses to give in. Stanley Hauerwas, author of *God, Medicine, and Suffering,* suggests that authentic lament is a biblical response to injustice: Lament is a tool that "God gives us to help us identify and respond to evil and injustice. For creation is not as it ought to be."[6]

Lament is a bold act of faith because it insists that every brokenness is a proper subject for God. Nothing is out of bounds— no emotion, no question, no doubt—because nothing can separate us from the love of God. We can bring all of the world's brokenness and our own sinfulness to the foot of the cross. "Everything," Brueggemann insists, "properly belongs in this conversation of the heart."[7]

The God of Israel, the God who tamed the seas and created the heavens, can handle your anger, your tears, and your questions. There is nothing you can do to make Him love you less. And He wants you. He wants you when you are angry. He wants you when you are tearful. He wants you when you are confused. He wants you when you doubt. He wants the *real* you.

The Israelites understood that God can handle our emotions. They believed that real communion with God was possible only when they brashly brought their complaints to Him. Israel's laments did not push away God; they brought Him close. The Is-raelites knew that the key to enduring suffering was to name it, to boldly bring every hardship to the One who chose them and anointed them.

As Stanley Hauerwas explains, lament can be formative. By bringing our hearts to God, we open ourselves to His working in and through our circumstances.

> The psalms of lament do not simply reflect our experience; they are meant to form our experience of despair. They are meant to name the silences that our suffering has created. They bring us into communion with God and one another, communion that makes it possible to acknowledge our pain and suffering, to rage that we see no point to it, and yet our very acknowledgement of that fact makes us a people capable of living life faithfully.[8]

Finally, lament is profoundly hopeful because it trusts God to do something. It's a forceful and powerful response to suffering because it acknowledges the brokenness of reality within the context of an all-powerful, all-loving Creator God. Lament is hopeful because it takes suffering to God, believing that He is active in the world, that He cares, and that He responds to those who call upon Him. Thus, for the Israelites, lament was typically composed of three phases: complaint, submission, and relinquishment.[9] They submitted their brash and unfiltered complaints to God and—this is key—relinquished them to Him with confidence.

Ultimately, lament is hopeful because of the gospel. Justice will come. Righteousness will reign. Every knee will bow and every tear will be wiped away by nail-scarred hands. Lament is profoundly hopeful because it recognizes that Jesus came to set the world right and will come again.

Children intuitively understand the genre of lament. They recognize and rage against injustice, large and small. And they bring those hurts, fears, and questions to their parents. Lament is possible for small children because it's directed at the caregivers they trust to set things right. Lament is possible because of faith.

Dr. Nathan Fox, director of the University of Maryland's Child Development Lab, tells a heartbreaking story. Fox studied children in Romanian orphanages. The babies suffered from severe neglect. They lay in their cribs day after day and were changed, bathed, and fed according to a set schedule. The babies were never rocked to sleep, never sung to, and never snuggled close. The startling thing about the infant room, Fox said, "was how quiet it was"; the infants "had learned that their cries were not responded to."[10] There was no lament because there was no hope.

When we look at lament through the lens of a well-loved child who expects, even demands, that a loving parent set things right, we see that authentic communication with our Father God is an act of faith. Stanley Hauerwas even suggests that there are serious theological problems with *not* expressing our emotions: "One of the profoundest forms of faithlessness is the unwillingness to acknowledge our inexplicable pain and suffering."[11] When we fail to bring our sorrow to the foot of the cross we are implicitly believing that God doesn't care, that He cannot help us, or that He (or our image of Him) needs protection from the reality of suffering.

Jesus on the cross shows us that nothing could be further from the truth. Jesus feels no need to protect God from His suffering and feelings of abandonment. "Eloi, Eloi, lama sabachthani?" (Mark 15:34, nasb)—"My God, my God, why have you forsaken me?" His authenticity is a bold challenge to God, a God from whom He feels distant, a God whom He no longer addresses as "Abba, Father" but as the more impersonal "God" of the Old Testament.[12] Yet even in His suffering and sense of abandonment, Jesus addresses God. His hope and confidence are implicit in the reality that Jesus expects to be heard. As John Swinton says, the crucified Jesus speaks into our suffering. "It's okay to feel this way," he writes. "God remains with you and for you despite what you are experiencing at this moment."[13]

Psalm 22 shows us how much the Lord values authenticity, how much He wants to hear the cry of your heart. In that psalm, David's searing honesty gives rise to one of the most poignant prophesies about the coming Messiah. It's incomprehensibly beautiful to me that by naming his suffering and taking it to God, David reveals God's plan of salvation: His Son on a cross.

In Psalm 22:1, David prophesied:

My God, my God, why have you forsaken me?

One thousand years later, Jesus echoed these very same words of isolation as He was crucified.

In Psalm 22:14, David prophesied:

I am poured out like water,
 and all my bones are out of joint;
my heart is like wax;
 it is melted within my breast.

One thousand years later, Jesus hung on the cross, His bones limp and His heart weak from pumping blood to distended limbs. In Psalm 22:15, David prophesied:

My strength is dried up like a potsherd,
    and my tongue sticks to my jaws.

One thousand years later, Jesus' fluids pooled in His lower extremities, a painful consequence of hanging on a tree. This posture causes an extremely dry mouth. As Jesus' tongue stuck to the roof of His mouth, He said in all of His humanity, "I thirst" (John 19:28). In Psalm 22:16 (NASB), David prophesied:

Dogs have surrounded me;
    A band of evildoers has encompassed me;
They pierced my hands and my feet.

One thousand years later, Jesus was surrounded by those who screamed, "Crucify! Crucify!" They pounded nails through flesh. The hands and feet of Jesus gave way. Those eternal holes are evidence, even today, of Christ's incomprehensible love. In Psalm 22:17, David prophesied:

I can count all my bones—
    they stare and gloat over me.

One thousand years later, Jesus was naked on a tree. His bones, all of them—His ribs, His hips, His ankles—were on display. In Psalm 22:18, David prophesied:

They divide my garments among them,
and for my clothing they cast lots.

One thousand years later, Roman guards divided Jesus' clothes, casting lots to see who might claim His tunic.

But even Psalm 22 is profoundly hopeful. A distraught King David went boldly to the throne of God with his complaints. David then invited the Lord into his suffering and asked for help: "O you my help, come quickly to my aid!" (Psalm 22:19). Finally, David relinquished his burden and ended on a note of certainty in God's deliverance. In another messianic foreshadowing, David prophesied about the day of salvation, a day when "the afflicted shall eat and be satisfied; . . . All the ends of the earth shall remember and turn to the LORD" (Psalm 22:26-27), a day when every knee will worship and proclaim Christ's righteousness, saying, "He has done it [that it is finished]!" (Psalm 22:31, AMPC).

One thousand years later, the King of kings traded in His righteousness for our unrighteousness and defeated the powers of sin, death, and darkness once for all. Again echoing Psalm 22, Jesus declared, "It is finished" (John 19:30). With those words, God's plan of salvation—His redemption and restoration of all who would call upon the name of Jesus, including you and me—was accomplished once for all.

David was childlike after the tradition of the Israelites; he went boldly to the throne with his questions, desires, and complaints. David was *real* with God. He took his deepest pain to the foot of the throne. And God honored him beyond measure by revealing

the Lord's plan of salvation for the waiting world through his
heartfelt plea.

We, too, can be honest with God. We can pray psalms of lament
and petition God to change our circumstances. We can be authentic
about our feelings, questions, doubts, and anger, and we can bring
them to the foot of the cross. We can ask the God of a thousand
stars to deliver us. And we can relinquish our burdens, certain of
that deliverance.

The poet Ann Weems wrote a psalm of lament to grieve the
death of her twenty-one-year-old son. Like King David, she is
searingly honest about her pain, bold in her request for shalom, and
finally able to relinquish her unbearable burden, testifying that her
God—and our God—is present in the darkness.

> O God, have you forgotten my name?
> How long will you leave me
> in this pit?
> I sang hosannas
> all the days of my life
> and waved palm branches
> greened in the new spring world.
> Rich only in promises
> from you
> I followed
> believing
>
> and then they killed him
> whom I loved
> more than my own life

(even that you taught me)
They killed him
whom you gave to me.
They killed him
without a thought
for justice or mercy,
and I sit now in darkness
hosannas stuck in my throat . . .

Why should I wave palm branches
or look for Easter mornings?
O God, why did you name me Rachel?
A cry goes up out of Ramah,
and it is my cry!
Rachel will not be comforted!
Don't you hear me,
you whose name is Emmanuel?
Won't you come to me?
How long must I wait
on this bed of pain
without a candle
to ward off the night?

Come, Holy One,
feed to me a taste of your shalom.
Come, lift to my lips
a cup of cold water
that I might find my voice

to praise you
here in the pit.
Pull forth the hosannas
from my parched lips
and I will sing to all
of your everlasting goodness,
for then the world will know that
my God is a God of promise
who comes to me
in my darkness.[14]

Have you ever personalized any of the psalms of lament, as Ann Weems did? Have you ever expressed yourself as David did in Psalm 22:2: "My God, I cry by day, but you do not answer, and by night, but I find no rest"? If not, why are you reluctant to do so? In the past, I've sometimes been reluctant to talk to God about the hurts or disappointments in my life, to express suffering or doubt, because to do so felt like faithlessness. If I know that God is good and intends good for me, I reasoned, then why should I complain to Him? Yet in this season of learning about childlike faith, God is showing me that, as a mother wants to know the heart hurts of her child, God wants me to tell Him about mine. He is teaching me how to share all of my thoughts and emotions with Him and showing me how to trust Him with my doubts and fears.

Dear one, it is okay to be real with God. In fact, this may be the most profound step of faith that you can take today. "Come to me," Jesus urges. "Come to me, now—just as you are. I want all of you. I want to hear about your hopes, your hurts, your disappointments, your confusion, and also your joy. I want to know how you really are. Please tell me about your day."

Jesus' invitation is unconditional; He wants a relationship with the real you. And that means bringing everything to His feet—your failures, your questions, and even your doubts—just as a child would.

Reflection Questions on Transparency

1. Do you find it difficult to be needy? Why or why not?

2. Write down any areas in your life in which you've been afraid to be honest with God or ask Him for help with a specific issue. Why do you feel this way? Can you be like King David, who modeled authentic communication?

3. If it seems difficult to start your own psalm of lament, use Psalm 13 as an example.
   a. Begin by expressing your hardship, doubt, or frustration. (v. 1-2)
      i. "How long, O LORD? Will you forget me forever?"
      ii. Tell God about your specific situation and how you feel about it.
   b. Petition the Lord, expecting Him to hear and answer you. (v. 3-4)
      i. "Consider and answer me, O LORD my God."
      ii. Present your specific request to the Lord.
   c. Relinquish your burden to the Lord, knowing He is trustworthy. (v. 5-6)
      i. "But I have trusted in your steadfast love; my heart shall rejoice in your salvation. I will sing to the LORD, because he has dealt bountifully with me."

4. How might authentic communication with God, complaining even, be a step of faith for you?

5. After you pray and ask God for help, are you able to relinquish the weight and worry to Him? Why or why not?

5

Embracing Fellowship

No longer do I call you servants . . .
I have called you friends.

—JOHN 15:15

"Why didn't Thomas want to hold my hand, Mom?" my three-year-old asked. We had been on a playdate with three other young boys. They'd all had a wonderful, rough-and-tumble time. On the way back to the parking lot, Elijah reached for the hand of his new friend. The friend, older and more sophisticated, refused to hold Elijah's hand. Elijah kept reaching out, grabbing the hand of his older friend. When it became obvious Thomas was having none of it, Elijah ran to Thomas's younger brother and offered his hand, only to be refused again.

"Why didn't Thomas want to hold my hand?" The question from the backseat contains the first glimmer of heart hurt that I can't kiss and cure. Elijah's question haunts me. And it causes me to ask questions of my own. Why does this broken world act so quickly, so decisively to squash the spontaneous openness of childlike love? Why does a three-year-old need to know what rejection feels like? And more practically, will my son reach out his hand again?

We often leave childhood authenticity behind as large and small rejections teach us the dangers of vulnerability. Critically, each rejection feeds the lie that we are alone, so we may learn to keep our cards close. We can become more self-reliant, learning to shut others out in order to protect ourselves. As we grow out of our childlike tendency to reach out spontaneously, as we seek to avoid rejection, we often learn to quiet our need for one another. That learned protectiveness extends to Christians as members of the church, too, even though we're meant to function as the body of Christ, with each part supporting the others.

Children are unselfconscious about their dependence on others and teach us that it's okay to need one another. They show us how to live as a church.

Holding Each Other's Hands

In addition to a relationship with Himself, God has given us a people. He has included us in a great nation, a veritable army of fellow believers. Fellowship with believers is a great source of comfort and joy, as John writes, "I hope to come to you and talk face to face, so that our joy may be complete" (2 John 12).

When we pray, we sometimes expect God to be obvious as He answers. We expect a parting of the waters, a calming of the wind, a water-to-wine moment. And God does work in miraculous ways. But He also directly works through His people.

In *How People Grow: What the Bible Reveals about Personal Growth*, Dr. Henry Cloud tells the story of his own healing from depression. He recalls being disappointed that healing had come primarily through other people—friends who took him in, loved him, and discipled him—and not directly from God. This sort of healing, Cloud recalls, seemed second-best, a Plan B that "felt more like sitting in the bleachers than the box seats."[1] He had wanted God to heal him miraculously, to zap him, even, and he'd had to "settle" for help from people instead.[2] Then Cloud had a life-changing realization: It was God who had healed him, in and through His people.

> [This understanding] helped me to realize that God was not far off and uninvolved, just delegating things to people. God did not delegate the process to people at all. He wore people as his uniforms. He came to live inside people and then lived out his wishes and will through them in a mystery called the Body of Christ. Jesus was with me all along by being in all of those people who were helping me. God was using his people as his Plan A.[3]

Sometimes people are God's Plan A. Peter tells us that we are to use our gifts to serve others "as good stewards of God's varied grace" (1 Peter 4:10). People, in other words, are ministers not only of kindness or friendship or fellowship, but of the very grace of God Himself.

We need the church. We need the church in the sense of a building where we come together and worship the risen Jesus. We need the church as a place where we learn more about God and His great love for us. But we also need the church in the sense of real human bodies. It isn't just that we need friendship but also that God is present in and through His people. God is with you by being in the people He uses to bring comfort, healing, or a good belly laugh. This is part of His Plan A.

RIGHT-HAND AND LEFT-HAND FRIENDS

Israel experienced a miraculous victory in Exodus 17. The nation was vulnerable—homeless and wandering in the wilderness—when they were attacked by the nation of Amalek. As the battle raged, Moses stood atop a nearby hill. So long as he held the staff of God high, the Israelites prevailed. But Moses grew weary; the effort was too much for him alone. His arms weakened, and as his hands sunk lower, the Amalekites began to win. But then Moses' friends stepped in. Aaron and Hur sat their friend on a stone to rest. They held up Moses' hands, one on each side, so that his hands remained steady until sunset. And the Israelites won the battle.

We are those Israelites. We have the Word of the Lord, and we have His Spirit, but we also need His church. We need His people. There are times when we need someone to hold up our right hand and someone to hold up our left hand so that we can fulfill the grand plans the Lord has designed just for us. As Exodus 17 shows us, these times are not only times of great trial but also times of great victory. We need people to intercede for us, to bring us and our prayers before the Lord.

We need this kind of friendship especially during difficult times. But the truth is that the battles of life are not just every now and again. Everyday life can *itself* be the battle, especially for moms of small children. We need one another every single day. We need support and encouragement. We need friends who see the best in us and who encourage us endlessly. We need friends who are honest about their struggles, because when they are, it makes us realize we are not alone in ours. We need our right-hand friend and our left-hand friend. And we need friends who will ask us how we really are.

RISKING FELLOWSHIP

I used to be one of the least transparent people I knew. Growing up, all I wanted was to be normal. We lived on a remote ranch in a county where the cattle outnumbered people forty to one (the ratio favors the cows even more now). I attended school with just under two hundred students, kindergarten through twelfth grade. In such a small community, there were no secrets. Everyone knew who had been at the only bar in town the night before (or every night in recent history). Everyone knew that my dad was an alcoholic.

One day Dad called to say he'd managed to rope a wild burro—and a beautiful paint at that. I fancied myself a horse whisperer and couldn't wait to have a chance to work with the little guy. But when one's life is lived under the influence of alcohol, not much turns out as planned. On Dad's way home, a hairpin turn proved too much after several drinks too many. Once, twice, the pickup truck flipped. Miraculously, someone drove by the remote area and pulled my father from the truck's unrecognizable frame.

We learned more about the wreck from a classmate at school the next day. Her mom was one of the paramedics at the scene of the accident. Still inebriated and in a state of shock, my dad repeatedly asked about the donkey colt—using terminology from the old

King James Version of the Bible. How is my a ___ ? Where is my a ___ ? etc. The paramedic and her daughter found this hysterical. Another classmate, whose parents owned the piece of property on which my dad's truck had crashed, remarked that the accident "sure tore up a lot of fence." Everyone had a story, and my sisters and I were celebrities of a sort the day after the accident. We seemed to be the subject of every whispered (and some non-whispered) conversation. All we wanted to do was disappear.

I thought that college was a place to start over. To be normal. A place where no one knew how messed up my family was, and by extension, how messed up I was. I managed to make it through college without talking much about my dad.

Several years after graduation, my best friend from college was helping my family gather cattle for springtime branding, an all-day affair. We'd been riding and talking most of the day when she cleared her throat and asked, "Can you tell me about your dad? You don't talk much about him." My breath caught in my throat. With her simple request, Hannah was telling me that she wanted to know the *real* me, not the façade that I so carefully maintained.

Hannah is the first person with whom I shared the story of my dad's alcoholism, depression, and suicide. The telling was painful, as long-buried feelings of shame bubbled to the surface. But there was also freedom. Her gentle question opened fissures in my heart that let in the healing love and light of Jesus. Her patient listening—her desire to know the real me—showed me that there is no shame in being damaged or broken (as we all are). For Jesus came to bind up the brokenhearted, to proclaim liberty to the captives, and to open wide the prison doors for those who are bound (Isaiah 61:1).

The real tragedy is trying to handle difficulty on our own,

something I still struggle with. I think of a tendency we can have as women to want to have it all together. One Bible study I was part of—we'll call it the "together" women's Bible study—comes to mind. (I don't mean to pick on our gender—maybe men have their "together" groups too—I just haven't been privy to them.) The group looks stunning; every hair is in place (except for mine), everyone is on time, and everyone shows up with the study questions answered and the text starred and highlighted. The undertone: Everyone's life is going pretty great.

When it's time for prayer requests, we ask for prayers for our great aunt Sally, who is battling cancer; for our best friend from high school, who is having a difficult time in her marriage; and for our neighbor's kids who, well, need lots of prayer. We pray for other people's battles, other people's marriages, and other people's children. And we leave feeling blessed to be a part of this with-it group.

Or, if you've been in a group like this, maybe you leave as I do: feeling alone. You leave realizing you *don't* have it all together. My need for a haircut pales in comparison to the desperation within: I need Jesus to live this life. And I need friends who remind me that Jesus is not afraid of my mess.

It's in isolation that our problems seem unbearably unique. I believe one of the most destructive lies that the devil tells us is that we are alone. Amidst all of the suffering that Mother Teresa saw, the greatest disease in the West was "being unwanted, unloved, and uncared for."[4] This is because we were created for relationship with Jesus and with one another. It's in fellowship that we see the love of the Lord—we see His hands reaching out. Part of the Lord's Plan A for your redemption and restoration involves His working through His people. And part of His Plan A to redeem and restore others involves Him working in and through you. He can use your deepest wounds to impart hope to others.

In *Still Waiting: Hope for When God Doesn't Give You What You Want*, Ann Swindell describes the shame she felt over a condition called trichotillomania, which in her case causes her to compulsively pull out her own hair, eyebrows, and eyelashes. She struggled in silence for decades, hiding her disease and its results from even her closest friends. Ann describes the decision finally to tell one of her dearest friends, Elsie. After she explained trichotillomania and that she'd struggled with it since childhood, there was mostly silence on the other end of the line. Ann continued, apologizing for having hidden this struggle from her friend: "I'm sorry I didn't open up this part of my life to you sooner."

"Oh, Ann," Elsie exclaimed, "I'm not upset. But my heart aches that I didn't know. I grieve that I couldn't walk with you through this trial, because you've walked with me through my valleys." Ann began to cry, too, realizing that her silence had caused them both hurt.[5]

When we fail to let those closest to us be part of our struggles, we deprive them of the opportunity to love—to be God's hands and feet. And when we are silent about our struggles, we feed the lie that we are alone.

Authenticity is one of the most overlooked weapons at the Christian's disposal, for it enables community. A childlike openness to love and to trust, the unselfconscious embrace of another, the risking of oneself in friendship and fellowship, the desire to participate in life together, even the gift of a messy house, of letting people in to see that your life is not Facebook perfect, directly counters the devil's plan to isolate us. Transparent and authentic relationships defeat the lie that we're alone.

In a Bible study years ago, one of the women made a surprising suggestion: During prayer time, we could only request prayer for ourselves. Seems odd, yes? A bit selfish? Definitely. Why would a group want to focus exclusively on the individual needs of its members? What about the pressing needs of the world around us? We ended up making exceptions for the critical needs of loved ones, but this general rule forced us to identify and to name the specific areas in which we personally and desperately needed the Lord's help. That honesty with each other, and with ourselves, created a deep bond. We asked for prayer for difficult situations. We prayed for engagements. Marriages. Job loss. Children. Singleness. The feeling that God was far away. Because we asked for the prayers that we really needed, we were able to shoulder one another's burdens, to laugh and to rejoice and to cry with one another. We were able to live life together because we were vulnerable.

It's still difficult for me to talk about my dad. But since my friend Hannah loved me into truth and light, I've come to see more of the good, to forgive more of the bad, and most importantly, to see the constancy of God's love in difficult circumstances. I may never know *why* some events occurred, but I do know *who* was there. And I know more of Jesus' heart for me, because of the people He's loved me through. I am learning that it's okay to need people.

LIFE TOGETHER

We were getting ready for a park playdate. I put the boys in their car seats and turned back to grab towels and an extra change of clothes. As I rushed to find clean socks, I heard the nails-on-chalkboard sound of toddler squabbling. I hurried out to see my then four-year-old (who never took a pacifier) gleefully sucking on his younger brother's beloved "paci." Blaise howled in anger. I unbuckled Elijah, plunked him down on a stool at our island counter, and instructed him to stay put until I found the missing socks. His howls of protest were no surprise. But Blaise's matching howls from the car were unexpected. A minute later, I put Elijah back in the car. Blaise, wreathed in smiles, turned to his brother and handed him his pacifier *and* blanket. He wanted Elijah's presence so much that he was willing to give up his most treasured possessions!

Dear friends, it's okay to need one another.

There are times in our lives when we can easily identify our right-hand friend and our left-hand friend. Maybe several of each. But there are also times when we move far away from our dearest friends, when we are in different life circumstances than those friends, or when we envy the friendships of others. In his book *Life Together*, Dietrich Bonhoeffer encourages those of us who desire more in the way of fellowship. He explains that Christian community is like sanctification. It is a gift. And only God knows the true state of our community: "What may appear weak and trifling to us may be great and glorious to God." Christian friendship, Bonhoeffer maintains, is not an ideal to work toward but "a reality created by God."[6]

> Christian brotherhood is not an ideal which we must realize; it is rather a reality created by God in Christ in which we may participate. The more clearly we learn to recognize that the ground and strength and promise of all our fellowship is in Jesus Christ alone, the more serenely we shall think of our fellowship and pray and hope for it.[7]

I love this picture of Christian fellowship—a reality created by God in which we participate. The strength and promise of our friendships are in Jesus Christ. We are bound together by a commonality that cuts across race, gender, and culture—the commonality of His Holy Spirit. We are a global people, a church that Jesus is growing for His glory. Christian friendship lets in the life and light of Jesus. And Jesus Himself tells us in no uncertain terms how powerful this fellowship is: "I will build My church; and the gates of Hades will not overpower it" (Matthew 16:18, NASB).

FELLOWSHIP WITH JESUS

We also have the friendship of Jesus. In John 15, Jesus explains that He has elevated us from the position of servant to that of friend: "No longer do I call you servants . . . I have called you friends" (John 15:15). The Greek word that Jesus uses here, *phílos*, means someone who is dearly loved in a personal, intimate way. Moreover, the root word *phil* focuses on experience-based love and personal affection. Jesus calls the disciples His friends because He knows and loves them in a personal, intimate way. Jesus ate with His friends, laughed with them, and shared their highest highs and their lowest lows.

I hope and pray that my two boys will grow up to be the closest of friends. And in between bouts of being fierce enemies, they show sparks of just such a relationship.

The boys love to race. They frequently zoom down the slight incline of our driveway. Just yesterday, Elijah sat astride a souped-up Big Wheel (Razor Riprider) and Blaise chose his trusty scooter. With loud whoops, the two took off down the driveway. Eyes glinting, heads down, feet pedaling/pushing furiously, the two kept abreast of one another. The most powerful thing about the scene was the boys' camaraderie: the playful competitiveness, the unpretentiousness, the simple enjoyment of each other. As I watch their carefree intimacy, I hear Jesus invite me into this sort of closeness with Him.

As my children enjoy one another, they are teaching me what it might look like to be friends with Jesus, or more accurately, to accept and live in the friendship that Jesus already offers to me. Sibling friendship can be particularly close and rewarding because brothers and sisters know the real us—all of the good *and* bad. So, dear ones, does Jesus. He is the friend who sticks closer than a brother. And He wants us to have enough confidence in His love that we can let down our guard and simply enjoy being with Him.

Jesus is the friend who desires our presence and laughter. He wants to cheer in delight with us as we race down the driveway together, simply because He adores our companionship. He is the friend with whom no pretense is needed, with whom we can leave it all and simply be. He is the friend who accepts us unconditionally, who sees in us His hard-won righteousness, who loves us without measure on our good days and on our bad.

This friend, this Jesus, knows us personally and wants us to come to Him with our highest highs and our lowest lows. This friend, this Jesus, will even come to wash dishes with us, turning shame and feelings of inadequacy into bubble splashes of joy and belonging. Dear one, listen to Him today as He calls you friend.

Jesus not only knows you intimately, He understands where you are coming from. The Bible tells us that Jesus suffered every humiliation.

As a mom, I am particularly overwhelmed by the thought of the little boy Jesus who was told He had a shameful, shady background. In a culture where lineage and family were everything, Jesus had a suspicious birth. His mother was an unwed pregnant teenager in a culture where infidelity by a woman was punishable by death.[8] Though Joseph's faithfulness spared Mary, tongues undoubtedly wagged. Nazareth was a tiny village of a few hundred people—a village where a pregnant girl would have stood out. In fact, throughout His ministry, the religious leaders seemed to question Jesus about His mother's character and the circumstances of His birth.[9]

Dear one, when you feel as if you don't belong, Jesus has been there. When you feel like an outcast, Jesus has been there. When you're looked down upon, told that you are less than, Jesus has been there. When you feel alone and ashamed, Jesus has been there. The very real child Jesus has been there.

It's no wonder that Jesus loved those whom society abused.

Jesus took those who were on the outside and brought them inside. The woman with the twelve-year hemorrhage is just one example. John MacArthur explains that the stigma and humiliation attached to her condition was second only to leprosy.[10] Because she never stopped bleeding, she was permanently unclean under Jewish law and excluded from everyday life. She couldn't have a relationship with her husband or care for her children (assuming she had either). She couldn't go to temple or otherwise participate in Israelite life. Anything and anyone she touched became unclean. Her condition resulted in absolute social and religious isolation. She had exhausted all of her resources on doctors (and probably a few charlatans). She was alone, destitute, and out of options.

And Jesus healed her in an instant. This woman whom society

had discarded believed that Jesus could make a difference: "If I only touch his garment, I will be made well," she said (Matthew 9:21). She crept close, shielding her face so people wouldn't recognize her, and grabbed hold of the tassel of Jesus' garment. Her life was radically transformed. She was instantaneously healed.

Jesus not only healed the woman, He restored her dignity. Perhaps recalling all of the childhood slights, all of the ugly-sounding names, all of the stigma He had endured as a young child, Jesus took compassion on the woman. He might easily have ignored her touch—after all, that touch likely made Him ceremonially unclean under Jewish law. But Jesus spoke directly to the woman. He spoke to her as a dear family member, as a beloved daughter, and commended her faith. He erased twelve long years of shame and embarrassment with His approval as He said, "Take heart, daughter; your faith has made you well" (Matthew 9:22). Without Jesus, the woman had been on the outside looking in. With Jesus, she belonged.

Without Jesus we are all on the outside looking in; we are all isolated from true community and true fellowship. But no matter our flaws and sinfulness, no matter our shame and embarrassment, Jesus invites us into fellowship with Himself and with all those who believe in Him. Will you embrace that fellowship today?

Reflection Questions on Embracing Fellowship

1. If there are parts of your story that you haven't shared with those closest to you, what's holding you back?

2. As you look back, can you see times when God has used people to heal and comfort you? Did this feel like second-best? Or could it be that this was God's Plan A—to show His love to you through other people? Are there ways you might be God's Plan A to help and encourage someone else today?

3. Do you see Jesus as your friend? Read John 15:15 to help remind you of the truth: Jesus calls you His friend. And He's waiting to spend the day with you, dear one.

6

Rest

Are you tired? Worn out? Burned out on religion?
Come to me. Get away with me and you'll recover
your life. I'll show you how to take a real rest. Walk
with me and work with me—watch how I do it.
Learn the unforced rhythms of grace. I won't lay
anything heavy or ill-fitting on you. Keep company
with me and you'll learn to live freely and lightly.

—MATTHEW 11:28-30, MSG

I often sneak into my boys' rooms to watch them as they sleep. There is something transcendent, something otherworldly, about sleeping children. Their faces are slack with peace. Snuggled up in footy pajamas, their chests rise and fall to unseen heartbeats. The four-year-old's arms are flung wide, covers strewn. The two-year-old is in a heap, face pressed into the bed, bottom up in the air. Despite their drastically different postures, there is a commonality of carefree abandonment. With each deep breath, the pent-up energy and tension from a day spent living at warp speed slips quietly away. In its place—perfect peace, complete contentment, shalom.

I'm fascinated by rest—probably because I don't get enough,

and neither do most people in this country. In 2013, the Centers for Disease Control and Prevention (CDC) identified insufficient sleep as a public health issue that leads to car crashes and industrial disasters. It decreases quality of life, increases mortality, and makes performing daily tasks difficult. It also contributes to hypertension, diabetes, depression, obesity, and cancer. Were the CDC's announcement about a new disease, we'd be searching hard to find a cure. We'd devote resources, create task forces, and have congressional hearings. Yet in America, we're so aware of our own sleep deficit we are immune to its statistics.

When we think biblically, the problem of insufficient sleep is even more acute than the statistics reveal. We've not only brushed off our need for sleep, we have forgotten entirely our need for rest.

One morning not long ago, I woke to the pitter-patter of small bare feet. It was just past 5:00 a.m. when two eyes suddenly appeared at eye level. "Mama, I can't sleep. Can you help me?" my four-year-old asked. As I climbed out of bed, he lifted his arms to be carried. We walked back upstairs, and he was fast asleep before his head hit the pillow.

As I watched Elijah sleep, his words kept going through my mind. "Mama, I can't sleep. Can you help me?" His simple statement and question have much to teach me about sleep. Small children unwittingly reveal the *theological* nature of rest.

First, rest is theological in that it admits we have limits. As my four-year-old acknowledged, we cannot survive without sleep. We sleep because we are finite. Second, rest is theological because it reveals a deep and abiding trust in a loving God. Rest is an abandonment of the world's work and worries to the One who never slumbers. Third, rest is theological when we recognize that it's a gift.

Rest as Limit

In the Jewish tradition, days do not begin with morning breaking new. They begin with the setting sun. This time inversion says something deeply theological. For the ancients, their days did not start with the morning rush out the door, packed lunches, homework slips, hasty breakfasts, and to-do lists. The day began in quiet acknowledgment of their limitations, their dependence on rest. This orientation of night first and day second puts the emphasis on God as Creator and human as limited participant. It is only once we succumb to rest that we may rise to join the Lord in what He has already started.[1] As Eugene Peterson says, "The Hebrew evening/morning sequence conditions us to the rhythms of grace. We go to sleep and God begins his work."[2]

When Martin Luther, the famous reformer, explained the theology of the cross, everything changed. At the heart of the theology is the idea that God achieves His purposes by doing the opposite of what humans expect. Nearly every core theological term of the time had to be redefined in light of this insight. Power, for example, referred not to human might but to strength hidden in weakness. The most compelling example: the cross itself. The seeming defeat and death of Jesus was actually the defeat of death itself.

As I think about rest, I wonder whether the theology of the cross applies here too—whether the Jewish culture has it right and whether, as the cross inverts all, we gain as we rest. Psalm 127:2 says as much: "It is in vain for you to rise up early, to retire late, to eat the bread of painful labors; for He gives to His beloved even in his sleep" (NASB). The Lord provides for us always—even, and maybe especially, as we rest.

By the time we are sixty, scientists say, we will have spent about twenty years asleep. My reaction to this statistic is one of absolute horror: *What a waste,* I think. *I could get a lot done in twenty years!* And yet it is impossible to go without sleep. Maybe that's the point. As Charles Spurgeon pithily remarked, "God gave us sleep to remind us that we are not him."[3] Sleep has deep theological significance because our need for it reveals the limitations of our own bodies, of our own humanity.[4]

And when we don't get enough sleep, these limits become apparent. I was sitting not long ago with a former student discussing her job application. She was asking about recommendation letters, and I suggested she ask a colleague whose name would *not* come to mind. From the time I was a small girl, I've been adept at remembering names and numbers, sequences and phrases. But no longer. The cumulative effect of two boys in two years (one who seems not to need sleep) had me grasping for the name of a well-known colleague (not to mention just the right word)!

And that's not its only effect: At times I intend to say something but hear something else entirely coming out of my mouth. Social situations are particularly tricky; when I'm especially tired, I enter them with trepidation, as I cannot tell whether or not I'm responding appropriately. My emotional-intelligence receptors have slowed to the point of nonresponse. And of course, as detailed by the CDC, sleep deprivation can have much more serious consequences. We drink coffee (or Diet Dr Pepper) by the gallon. But at some point, our strength runs out. *We* run out.

It's humbling to think that even Jesus needed rest. Scripture tells us that "as often as possible Jesus withdrew to out-of-the-way places for prayer" (Luke 5:16, MSG). These moments of quiet, of covenantal communion, of rest, were prioritized. Important work and a demanding schedule were no excuse: Jesus fitted the world's most impactful ministry into three intense years, and yet He rested as often as possible. His days of teaching, preaching, and healing were bookended by—held up by—these moments of rest. As Henri Nouwen writes of this verse,

> In the center of breathless activities, we hear a restful
> breathing. Surrounded by hours of moving, we find a mo-
> ment of quiet stillness. In the heart of much involvement,
> there are words of withdrawal. In the midst of action, there
> is contemplation. And after much togetherness, there is
> much solitude.5

It was in withdrawal, in rest and communion with the Father God, that Jesus was refreshed and encouraged. It was in the stillness and quietness that Jesus was, and we are, filled. Psalm 46:10 urges us to "be still, and know that I am God." The two clauses are related, interdependent even. In order to fully know God, we must be still. In order to comprehend His majesty, to soak in His love, to see His hand amidst creation and in our fellow man, we must be still. We must rest.

In the face of so much frenetic activity and American focus on productivity, prescient voices have been suggesting that sleep might be a spiritual discipline.[6] Take this admonition from D. A. Carson:

> Sometimes the godliest thing you can do in the universe is
> get a good night's sleep—not pray all night, but sleep. I'm
> certainly not denying that there may be a place for praying

all night; I'm merely insisting that in the normal course of things, spiritual discipline obligates you to get the sleep your body needs.[7]

To think of rest and sleep as spiritual disciplines upends my too-often work-based theology. If I were to list the "godliest thing" that I might be doing, a good night's sleep would not even be on the list. But I think my children (not to mention D. A. Carson) are onto something. As Tish Harrison Warren puts it, "For Christians, the act of ceasing and relaxing into sleep is an act of reliance on God."[8] This letting go of our own efforts, this abandonment of the world's work and worries, the ability to let our faces collapse into perfect peace, is theological. Our bodies were created to need rest, and there is something deeply symbolic (as well as practical) about acknowledging our need.

Rest as Abiding

It was *almost* comical. Without fail, when Blaise was about six weeks old, he would start awake at five o'clock every morning. He would scrunch his face, shake his fists (if he'd escaped his swaddle, which was frequently the case), and squirm. The poor little guy would have gas—and lots of it. I would wait, hoping he would settle. Most nights it had been a little over an hour since he'd eaten, and I would have just fallen back to sleep. The mothers reading this know the drill.

And did I mention he was loud? He grimaced and groaned and made the occasional sound of relief. Before you feel too sorry for him, however, I must let you in on a little secret: Something miraculous happened when I picked him up. Within seconds, the groans would subside and be replaced with the deep rhythmic breathing of the very young. Blaise would be out cold—until I began inching toward the bassinet. That's when the groans would make a startling reappearance. I'm not sure how my holding of him actually relieved physical digestive discomfort, but one thing was certain: My baby rested peacefully when he was in his mom's arms.

Biblical rest is much more than sleep. In Mark 6, Jesus sent the disciples out in pairs to proclaim the gospel, cast out demons, and heal the sick. And they did. They came back utterly exhausted. They had been so busy bringing light and life to the world that they didn't have time even to eat. The disciples needed a hot meal and a long nap—yet Jesus did not send them away to rest. Rather, seeing their bone-deep exhaustion, Jesus invited them to come to Him: "Come away . . . and rest a while" (Mark 6:31). Explaining this verse, Priscilla Shirer highlights Jesus' instructions: Jesus did not command His disciples to go away but to come with Him. When we are all poured out, the key to true rest is to draw near to Jesus.

Dear one, I get it. Sometimes the days are too short and rest is only a nice-sounding theory. Long ago Jesus, too, was tired. He was surrounded by people who needed Him even more desperately than they knew. They were constantly looking to touch Him, to be healed by Him, to be fed by Him, to learn from Him. He was literally their only shot at life, their only possible Savior. The crush of their neediness forced Him to teach from the safety of an offshore boat and to withdraw to quiet places as often as possible. And then there were those who interrogated Him, who sought to find fault, who paid others to lie about Him.

In the midst of all these demands, it might just be that Jesus didn't always get eight uninterrupted hours of sleep. Jesus sat at the well because He was weary (John 4:6). In all of His humanity, Jesus was flat-out exhausted. Yet Jesus was *always* at rest in the Father. The key to rest for Jesus was coming to the Father. So too with us. "Come to me," Jesus promises, "and I will give you rest" (Matthew 11:28).

One word that helps capture the rest that Jesus enjoyed is *abide*. The original Greek word for abide, *meno*, can be translated "remain, abide, stay, dwell, or wait." All of these verbs have at their common core the idea of protective connectedness: the idea that abiding is a passive but powerful sort of activity that depends upon an intimate relationship with a third party. Abiding reminds me of a six-week-old's rhythmic breathing—infants sleep best when they are held close, when they are intimately connected to their parents.

Jesus invites us to "abide in" Him (John 15:4). This is one of my favorite biblical invitations. Jesus is saying, "Remain in me. Wait in me. Stay in me. Dwell in me. Be connected to me." Eugene Peterson paraphrases it this way in *The Message*: "Live in me. Make your home in me just as I do in you" (John 15:4).

Children abide in their parents in a very clinical way. Young ones, psychologists say, don't understand that they exist separately. Newborns think they are simply an extension of their moms—thus, their extreme distress when Mom is unavailable. They abide in every sense of the word. They literally believe that their mom *is* their home.

We are invited into just this sort of connectedness. We are invited to make our home in Jesus, just as He does in us. Dear daughter of Christ, listen as the King Most High invites you to abide in Him. To remain in His love. To wait in His love. To rest in His love. To make your home in Him—where nothing can separate you from His vast love.

I've mentioned my boys' knee-check before, but for me it is an example of what it looks like to abide in Jesus. The boys are busy going about their everyday tasks. They zigzag about the playground or jump in the bounce house, but every so often they glance back. They run to me and give my legs a full body hug. They snuggle their faces in my knees, resting for a moment in the security my love provides, and then they are off again. This example is imperfect; since Jesus is always with us, we don't need to run back to Him. But my boys show me how to make a conscious effort to check in with Jesus as I go about my daily work. I can look to Him, remember to talk to Him, rest for a moment in His favor, and receive His reassurance throughout my day.

Abiding is the place of our fruitfulness, where we bloom and flourish. It's where we pause and, in the stillness, take a deep breath and let our guards down. It's the place where we allow our roots to sink deep into relationship with Jesus, where we accept His invitation and open our arms to His presence. Abiding is the place where we sit with Jesus—just sit with Him—and soak in Him. It's the still place of restful, rhythmic breathing, the place where we lie down and sleep because the Lord sustains us.

As moms, it can be difficult to acknowledge our finiteness. We are always needed by someone. But dear one, please hear me. The most important thing you can do for your child today is to grow in your relationship with Jesus. Full stop. There is nothing that will make you a better mom than getting to know Jesus more. On occasion that may mean letting your kids watch thirty minutes of *Paw Patrol* so you can do your morning devotion. It may mean asking your spouse or a family member to watch your babies so you can attend a women's conference. It may mean asking your children to play quietly while you pray. I think of Susanna Wesley, mom to the enormously influential preacher John and his songwriter brother Charles, who found a way to pray (reportedly for hours!) while mothering a household of children. She would sit in the chaos and flip her apron over her head! Her children knew not to disturb her; she was talking to Jesus. In the midst of motherhood, Susanna knew the importance of resting in Jesus.

Indeed, Jesus teaches us that to abide in Him is the *only* way to bear fruit. All of our labors are in vain unless we are joined to Jesus. This was true even for Jesus, who said, "I can do nothing on my own. . . . I seek not my own will but the will of him who sent me" (John 5:30). For Jesus, it was His Father God who was at work: "The words that I say to you I do not speak on my own authority, but the Father who dwells in me does his works" (John 14:10). When we make our home in Jesus, we are able to rest. We accept our limitations, we leave the results of our God-given work to Him, and we trust Him to sustain us.

King David, the man after the Lord's own heart, also had a childlike ability to rest. In one of the Bible's saddest tales of family dysfunction, David's son Absalom sets out to kill his father and usurp his throne. He nearly succeeds. David is forced to flee, leaving Jerusalem. He is vulnerable and heartbroken, surrounded by friends-turned-enemies on every side.

Yet the Bible tells us that King David lies down and he *sleeps*. Can you imagine? If I were in David's shoes, I'm pretty sure sleep would not come easily—or at all. I'd be awash in grief, remorse, fear, and relentless, swirling questions: "Why? Why? What did I do wrong? How can I fix this?" For me, worry and grief surely would mingle into a toxic, sleepless brew. But King David lies down like a small child. And he sleeps.

Psalms 3 and 4 tell us his secret. King David has a childlike confidence in God that even betrayal and treachery cannot touch. He cries out to God, and then 100 percent sure of God's covenantal protection, he sleeps. David's complete dependence on the Lord is life-giving: "I lay down and slept; I woke again, for the LORD sustained me," he writes (Psalm 3:5). Faith makes rest possible: "In peace I will both lie down and sleep; for you alone, O LORD, make me dwell in safety" (Psalm 4:8).

Further, King David makes a studied contrast between rest and action. David relinquishes control. He assumes the defenselessness of sleep because he anticipates *divine* action. David can sleep because he expects the Lord to "arise" and deliver him (Psalm 3:7). I love this imagery of waking—of arising. In this psalm about unexplainable peace in the midst of extreme hardship, David leaves the action to God. David retires, but it is the Lord who awakes, the great I Am who arises to go forth and fight the battle.

When we sleep, when we surrender our physical safety as well as our work, our worries, and our plans, we trust in the Lord to arise. Like a baby sleeping in her mom's arms, David trusts fully in his Father's ability to protect him, to go forth and fight the battle for him—and we can too.

I have a confession to make. I know what real rest looks like because I have experienced it a lot on Sundays—during church! For the last few years, sleep has proven elusive. Our two boys would wake early and often during their first few years, and thyroid issues meant I'd lie awake even when the babes were sleeping. I know my wakefulness is far from uncommon; millions of women suffer from much more serious sleep disorders every year. And if this is you, know you are not alone. My prayers are with you—prayers for real rest, for nights of uninterrupted sleep, and for mornings waking fresh.

Sunday morning would dawn after nights of intermittent sleep. My eyes inevitably would grow heavy as our pastor opened up Scripture. My husband was not above the occasional elbow, but the allure of rest was strong. I was embarrassed by my closing eyelids but also curious. What was it about church, in particular, that allowed me to sink into sleep when rest otherwise proved so elusive?

One morning, I realized the twofold reason for my Sunday sleepiness: I was exactly where I was supposed to be and I had no other responsibilities. My children were tucked away in kid wonderland learning about Jesus. The laundry was miles out of reach. My cell phone was tucked out of sight—no checking for work emails or text messages from friends. On Sunday mornings, I was given permission to cease the worry and the work. I was given the gift of simply abiding in Jesus. Though I don't recommend sleeping through sermons(!), I do wish for us all an abiding place, a place where we can sit quietly in Jesus' presence and simply be at home.

The place doesn't need to be fancy and the time doesn't need to be long. I once heard someone describe their "quiet time" as coffee with their best friend, Jesus. I love this description and have tried to put it into practice. Dear one, when you have five minutes in the morning (when the reality of motherhood doesn't interrupt), curl up with a blanket and a hot cup of coffee or tea. As the blanket surrounds you, sit back and exhale. Imagine yourself sitting next to your dearest friend: the friend from whom you hide nothing, who knows you inside and out, loves you dearly, and just wants to spend time with you. Refuse to scroll through your phone. Instead, let yourself be held by Him. Listen to Him. Sit quietly, expecting His still small voice to speak life into your soul. And when a thought distracts, take the thought and give it to Jesus. Relinquish the worry. God is the God who never slumbers so that *we* can. Like David, pray about your situation and then let it go, dear sister. Give it to Jesus.

REST AS FREEDOM

In our children's ability to combine rest with joy, we see the giftedness of rest. We see that biblical rest brings freedom. I'm reminded of the difference between playing possum and actually sleeping. When my eldest pretends to be sleeping, or plays possum, it's pretty obvious. He screws his eyes shut and squinches his face. His body is rigid with effort. Truth be told, he looks a lot more like someone in excruciating pain than someone resting. But when he actually falls asleep, the change is instantaneous and dramatic. His face smooths. His eyelids droop and his muscles unwind. His fervent efforts to produce sleep are overcome by the reality of sleep.

For me, rest can seem like effort, like playing possum with my eyes scrunched and body tense. But the Bible teaches us that rest is a gift from the Father of lights. The God of creation did not model rest on the seventh day to impose greater demands upon His beloved people but to set them free to enjoy Him. Isaiah 58 explains the purpose of the Sabbath prohibition on work so that the delighted-in creation might delight in their Creator.

> "If you watch your step on the Sabbath
> and don't use my holy day for personal advantage,
> If you treat the Sabbath as a day of joy,
> God's holy day as a celebration,
> If you honor it by refusing 'business as usual,'
> making money, running here and there—
> Then you'll be free to enjoy God!
> Oh, I'll make you ride high and soar above it all.
> I'll make you feast on the inheritance of your ancestor Jacob."
> Yes! God says so!
> (Isaiah 58:13-14, msg)

Sabbath was made to be a day of joy. Sabbath was made to be a day of celebration. We honor God when we stop looking for an advantage, when we take a break from business as usual. As we do so, we become free to worship and to enjoy God.

God created the Sabbath for us, and in order to know how to celebrate it, in order to be free to enjoy God, we must know what gives us joy. To observe Sabbath, Brady Boyd writes, "You've got to know what makes you come alive."[9] When we wake exhausted, it can be hard to remember what makes us feel alive. If that's the season you are in now, I feel your pain. Start slow. Take a walk. Scrapbook. Take an honest-to-goodness nap. Sit still, even if it's only for five uninterrupted minutes.

Brady Boyd writes convincingly about "bedhead days," days when he and his family lounge and rest and play and sleep in.[10] My husband was in a particularly busy season of life when he read about these bedhead days and announced that the next Saturday he was taking a theological break—a bedhead day. Now, I admire the principle and look forward to practicing it someday, a day in which our kids are not up early and often. But Josh's bedhead day meant I was alone with the kids in the morning. Again. They were early risers, so by the time Josh's bedhead morning actually started, we'd been up for hours. Needless to say, bedhead mornings were not altogether popular around our house.

Now, instead of a bedhead day, my husband almost always takes the boys out on Saturday mornings. They go to the donut shop and then to run off their sugar high at the gym. This mom has hours of uninterrupted time—of Sabbath. I read. I walk. I pray. I enjoy the sunlight on the grass. But I also clean up in peace, which feels like rest. And I write, which feels like grace. These things, friends, can be a sort of Sabbath when we are still before the Lord, when we accept His invitation to spend time with Him, to abide in Him. As a matter of fact, both Brady Boyd and Mark Buchanan—two pastors who have written extensively about rest—admit to mowing the grass on the Sabbath because they enjoy it!

The Pharisees would have been appalled. But D. A. Carson explains how the religious leaders of the day had turned God's gift of rest into a burden.

Instead of understanding it to be their privilege to rest on Sabbath, they viewed it as a deprivation. Instead of recognizing their opportunity to commune with God, they saw only inconvenience and hardship. Rather than discovering freedom to worship, they felt in bondage to a law, and instead of grasping the idea of renewal of their covenant relationship to God, they experienced the tragedy of legalism.[11]

In commanding the Israelites to observe Sabbath, God meant to grant them freedom.[12] He gave them freedom to cease from ordinary work, to put aside their questions about budgets, work deadlines, paying rent—and even their concern for eight uninterrupted hours of sleep. He offered them freedom to spend time with and enjoy the God who foreknew them before the world began, the God who fashioned them in their mothers' wombs, the God who loved them so much He sent His only Son to die a ghastly death as payment for their sins.

Scripture tells us that God gave Sabbath to the Israelites in part to remind them they had been set free. The Lord instructed His people to keep the Sabbath day, so that "you shall remember that you were a slave in the land of Egypt, and the LORD your God brought you out from there with a mighty hand and an outstretched arm" (Deuteronomy 5:15).

Egypt looked pretty safe. For the set-free Israelites, the unknowns of wilderness liberty were too much. They wanted to go back to Egypt, to slavery. The Egypt to which I return can look like self-sufficiency and busyness. It can look like the efforts of my hands. But Sabbath reminds me that it is through Jesus that we are set free. As Mark Buchanan writes, Sabbath is "a condition of liberty" and "a refusal to go back to Egypt."[13]

As my little possum turns sleeping child, I see firsthand the freedom in rest. I hear Jesus say, "Are you tired? Worn out? Burned out on religion? Come to me. Get away with me and you'll recover your life" (Matthew 11:28, MSG). Dear one, hear Jesus today: "Come away by yourselves to a secluded place and rest a while" (Mark 6:31, NASB). "I'll show you how to take a real rest. Walk with me and work with me—watch how I do it. Learn the unforced rhythms of grace. I won't lay anything heavy or ill-fitting on you. Keep company with me and you'll learn to live freely and lightly" (Matthew 11:28-30, MSG).

The invitation to experience true rest—to walk with Him and to work with Him, to learn the unforced rhythms of grace—is always extended.

Now for the truth. Writing this chapter makes me feel like a fraud. I'm writing about something I struggle to possess but do not. The characteristics that are intrinsic to children—joy, desire for relationship, courageous living, and authentic transparency—each of them challenges me, deeply. But rest, *rest* is particularly elusive. To me, rest feels like a relinquishment, a letting go of control. In rest, I'm forced to recognize my limits, that I simply cannot do it all. And of course, that's the point. But letting go of my own efforts is frightening. And rest often also feels impossible. Between night terrors, winter flus, summer colds, and our family's travel-heavy schedule, my children are up frequently. My inoperative thyroid also contributes to sleepless nights. But even more than this, I find it difficult to leave it all—unfinished as it is—in the hands of the One who made it all. For me, it's challenging to realize as the ancients did that my day starts with a closing of the eyes, with a turning over of all of my hopes, dreams, and plans to Jesus, and that as I close my eyes, the Father God goes to work.

Dear one, I'm praying that together we might become childlike in our rest, that we might be at peace with our finiteness and leave our work and worry to David's God—the God who never slumbers but arises. Let's pray that we'll find freedom in rest, and that as we keep company with Jesus, we'll learn to live freely and lightly.

Reflection Questions on Rest

1. Are you tired? Worn out? Or burned out with all that is on your plate? The King of kings invites you to come to Him and experience true rest. Ask Jesus to teach you how to rest as you abide in Him.

2. What things or attitudes prevent you from being able to experience true rest? Ask God to give you wisdom.

3. What are some practical ways that you can abide in Jesus in the midst of a busy day? Can you turn on a worship song as you clean the kitchen and listen to Jesus as you wipe down countertops? Can you take a short walk—with Jesus? Can you limit social media and email to a certain time of day so you can do a knee-check with Jesus instead of checking your phone? That's what I'm trying to do.

4. How does seeing the Sabbath's command as one of enjoying the Lord change your view of the day? What activities or experiences make you come alive? How can you practice Sabbath by incorporating them into the day?

7

Bold Requests

*Then you will call upon Me and come and pray to Me,
and I will listen to you. You will seek Me and find
Me when you search for Me with all your heart.*

—JEREMIAH 29:12-13, NASB

Round and golden, the moon hung low over the horizon. We
had returned home late from a visit to Nana's house, and my
two-year-old son was enjoying the last slanting light of the summer
sun. Then he noticed the moon. "Mama, what *is that*?" my incredulous toddler asked. His bedtime schedule meant that he rarely, if
ever, saw the summer moon. Entranced, Elijah stood stock-still.
And then he jumped, fingers outstretched, reaching for the golden
globe. And he jumped. And he jumped.

Finally, he turned to me in exasperated disbelief. "I can't reach
it. Mama, will you get it for me?"

There was not even a hint of doubt in his eyes. My two-year-old
was certain that I not only could produce the moon but would. It
nearly broke this mama's heart to tell him, "I'm sorry, Elijah; I can't
reach the moon either."

"Mama, will you get it for me?" Children are not shy of making wild requests of their parents. As we get older we often learn to lower our expectations and to be more timid in pursuing the deepest desires of our hearts. While a dose of reality can be a good thing, children show us the Lord's heart for our prayers. They show us how to make outrageous requests, to believe that our prayers will be heard and answered, and to never, *ever* give up.

OUTRAGEOUS REQUESTS

The Bible is full of outrageous requests. Particularly outrageous for the time was the brave Canaanite woman in Matthew 15. She was a mom with a troubled daughter. She was a woman during a time period when women were less than. They were not allowed to speak to men in public, and their testimony was considered so unreliable that they were not allowed to serve as witnesses in legal cases. Canaanite women were in an even worse position. The Israelites and Canaanites were forbidden from intermarrying and constantly at war.

Yet this woman boldly approached Jesus and cried out to Him for help. She didn't care who heard her or what they thought. Even when Jesus failed to answer (some nonanswers to prayers are actually Jesus saying "wait, my darling, just wait"), the woman refused to give up. She kept it up so long and was so loud and distracting that the disciples urged Jesus to send her away.

When Jesus finally spoke, His words were not encouraging. Jesus told the Canaanite woman that He was sent only to the lost sheep of Israel. Even this did not deter the brave mom: "Lord, help me," she responded (Matthew 15:25). Then, knowing the depth of this brave woman's faith, Jesus replied, "It is not right to take the children's bread and throw it to the dogs" (verse 26). Still undeterred, she said, "Yes, Lord, yet even the dogs eat the crumbs that fall from their masters' table" (verse 27). Upon this amazing display of confident belief, Jesus spoke words to her that live on through time immortal: "O woman, great is your faith! Be it done for you as you desire" (verse 28). Her daughter was healed at that very instant.

The Canaanite woman's request was outrageous. As a woman, it was culturally taboo for her to speak to a man in public. On top of that, she was not even Jewish. And yet this brave mom asked for the impossible.

And Jesus answered.

While Jesus' initial reaction may at first blush seem less than charitable, Jesus knew who was standing before Him. He knew the Canaanite woman inside and out. He knew her strength, the depth of her childlike faith, and her great love for her daughter. He knew she would persevere and provide an encouraging example to this mom two thousand years later. I'm humbled by her example, the mom who dared public ridicule to reach out with both hands and ask for a miracle. In her bold asking, as in Elijah's request for the moon, I see the Father's heart for us: the boldness to ask, to really ask, for our hearts' desires.

ASKING AS A DAUGHTER

A toddler's freedom in making an outrageous request—Can I have the moon? Can I have ice cream for breakfast? Can I have a *real* sword?—comes from their identity *as a child*. They don't ask random strangers for the moon. Nor do they pepper even close relatives with a never-ending stream of requests and demands. Children's comfort in requesting so much so often depends upon their relationship with the person whom they are asking. They ask because they are daughters and sons.

This, dear friend, is how Jesus prayed—as a son to His father. This is how He teaches us to pray too. In the Lord's Prayer, Jesus famously instructs His disciples to begin their prayers with the invocation "Our Father who is in heaven" (Matthew 6:9, NASB). The original Greek, pater, means "begetter, creator, progenitor, one in intimate connection and relationship." In the Old Testament God is referred to as the Father of the nation of Israel but seldom of individuals. Jesus changes all of that. He gives us the right to call God our Father in the personal, individual sense—He is the Father God of "intimate connection and relationship." He is our begetter and our creator.

Even more, through Jesus we can claim the God of the universe as our "Abba," our papa or daddy. There has been some academic debate as to whether *Abba* really should be translated to mean "daddy or papa." Regardless, the word is unquestionably an affectionate, tender endearment between child and father. It comes from the root word *pa*, which means "nourisher, protector, upholder." Galatians tells us that God sent forth the Spirit into our hearts to cry, "Abba! Father!" (Galatians 4:6). And Paul especially picks up on this close relationship, explaining that we have been given a spirit of adoption, whereby we too may cry, "Abba! Father!"

I love how children naturally refer to special things in the diminutive. Elijah's younger brother, Blaise, becomes Blaisie; his special blanket, Love, becomes Lovey; Mom, becomes Mommy. That special word *Mommy* gets my attention more than any other. It arises out of relationship and makes a claim upon me. My boys can call out to me morning or night because they are mine. It was not so long ago that these gifts of life were miracles nestled inside me, eating the food I ate, breathing the air I breathed. My boys can refer to me as Mama, Mommy, or even as they get older, *Mom!* because of our close relationship.

Through our adoption in Jesus, we have just this sort of intimate relationship with the God of the universe. He is our closest ally. He is our stronghold. He is our nourisher, our protector, and our upholder. He knit us together in our mothers' wombs. He provides the food that we eat and the air that we breathe. He delights in us and He gives us life. We can pray to Jesus out of the same sort of expectation, born of a loving and trusting relationship, that allows our children to request the moon, or even a third lollipop.

Hearing and Answering

"Mom, I'm hungry. Mom, can I have some juice? Mom, can I have some Goldfish? Mom, can I go outside? Mom, can I go inside? Mom, can I dig up your flowers (oops)? Mom, can we do an experiment? Mom, can you help me go potty? Mom, can we watch *Ready Jet Go?* Mom, can you read me a story? Mom, can Peter come over? Mom, can we go to the park? Mom, can we go exploring?"

Mom. Mom. Mom. The requests—from the quite reasonable to the truly bizarre—never stop coming. There are the big demands: "Mama, can I have the moon?" And there are the everyday ones: "Mama, can you hold me?" Small children do not distinguish among gradations of requests. They do not hesitate to ask for the grand or the mundane. And there are times when a child doesn't even know the difference between the two. And that is okay. A friend of mine with a new baby recalls her four-year-old, probably feeling the sting of sharing Mom with a younger brother, yelling "Mom, come now; it's an *emergency*." The emergency? A torn paper towel. But that mom came anyway; she responded to her child's earnest ask.

Our children do not hesitate to make demands upon us, for they know we will hear and answer. There is something wonderful about the boldness of a child's request. It's biblical, after all. As John, the beloved disciple, tells us, "This is the confidence that we have toward him, that if we ask anything according to his will he hears us" (1 John 5:14). No matter how big or seemingly insignificant the request, God hears us.

Our children can remind us of this fact. One day, Blaise fell and hit his head. I was worried and asked Elijah to pray with me for protection and healing. Later that day, as we were saying our nightly prayers, I again asked Elijah to pray for his brother. With the exasperated tone of a four-year-old going on sixteen, he replied, "But Mom, we already prayed for that." For Elijah, we had asked, and the Lord had undoubtedly answered. And that was that.

But we grow up. Along with age comes doubt. And most of us are less than childlike in our earnest expectation that the One who loves us best *actually* hears and answers. Because His disciples were also adults who tended toward doubt, Jesus reassured them no fewer than *six* times in two verses that the Lord hears and answers.

> And I tell you, *ask*, and it will be given to you; *seek*, and you will find; *knock*, and it will be opened to you. For everyone who *asks* receives, and the one who *seeks* finds, and to the one who *knocks* it will be opened. (Luke 11:9-10, emphasis mine)

I love how the *Amplified Bible* translates Luke 11:9 (emphasis mine): "Ask and *keep on asking*...; seek and *keep on seeking*...; knock and *keep on knocking*." With all of His emphasis on persistence, it almost sounds as if Jesus had a toddler in mind.

Incessant asking is deeply biblical because it shows us the right relationship between petitioner and petitionee: one of dependency. Children ask, "Will you give me x, y, and z?" They don't say (at least until they hit their independent streak) "I will get x, y, and z." Their asking acknowledges a relationship of reliance, trust, provision, and fellowship. It concedes a higher power. By asking, children admit that, however badly they might want something, they are powerless to attain that something. It is beyond their grasp. By asking, children recognize that they are not fully independent. And neither are we.

Of course, God knows our wants and our needs. He is more intimately familiar with the deepest desires of our hearts than those hearts are themselves. But the Bible nevertheless tells us that God wants us to come before Him and *ask*. As Charles Spurgeon puts it, "Asking is the rule of the kingdom."[1] Our children show us the reason: Asking places God in His proper position as giver and us in the proper position of receiving daughter. As parents ourselves, don't we teach and expect our children to ask for the things they desire? Similarly, God wants us to ask Him in the same way. Yet it is difficult to pray sometimes.

As a mom, there's just so much to do. Laundry, dishes, meal prep, serving, work assignments, actually talking to your husband, sweeping the kitchen floor (again), taking a meal to the new mom in your Bible study, and the list goes on and on. The enemy would love to distract us with all of these things—to keep us so busy *doing* that we forget to talk to God. But this, dear sister, may be our most important work: to pray for our husbands, to lift up our daughters and our sons, to bring the Lord our hearts' desires.

❧

Enoch is listed as one of the heroes of the faith. He along with the prophet Elijah are the only two people who skipped death as a reward for well-lived lives. What was Enoch's great accomplishment? To become childlike. Enoch is a hero of the faith because he approached God with childlike confidence believing that God existed and that He cared enough to respond to those who sought Him (Hebrews 11:6).

In our lean-in world, we are so often encouraged to take charge, to never say no to an assignment, and to act as if we have it all under control. There's no doubt that God wants us to steward our gifts and talents and to have confidence. But we are to have *transcendent* confidence—the confidence of a beloved daughter, who achieves *because of* and *in* and *through* our Lord. We're to have the assurance of a daughter who knows—regardless of any particular outcome— that she's an irreplaceable part of an even larger story. This daughter knows she's valuable because she *is*, not because she *does*.

No matter the circumstance in which you find yourself today, you can bestow a gift of incomprehensible worth on those you love: the invaluable gift of prayer. At an event before Josh and I were married, one of my mother-in-law's good friends took me aside and with tears in her eyes told me a story about the carpet in my mother-in-law's bedroom. The carpet had been pressed down and worn out by praying knees. I'm undone by the picture of a carpet growing more and more threadbare, day after day. My mother-in-law covered her son and her daughter in prayer. She prayed about their well-being, bodies and souls. She prayed about the big things and the small things. She prayed when she was worried and when she was overjoyed. She prayed when she didn't know what to do, and she prayed when she thought she knew the answer. She asked, and she had the confidence of a child to keep asking.

I remember my mother-in-law telling me a story of a time she felt prompted to pray repeatedly for her son's wife. Now, the story is a little strange because Josh was only seven or eight years old at the time! The story is also incredibly powerful because that time period was especially difficult for my family. I know the Lord heard those prayers and answered them. He protected and preserved my sisters and me from the chaos and upheaval of addiction, depression, and divorce in part because of her prayers. As the Bible reminds us, "The prayer of a righteous person [and that means us in Jesus] has great power as it is working" (James 5:16, insertion mine).

Another mom recently told me how, due to difficult circumstances, she's been forced to pray specifically. That specificity has been a blessing, she said, because her eyes have been opened to see the Lord's answers to detailed prayer requests. Her words encourage me to be specific in my prayers too.

Today I'm praying especially that my young ones would get along (we need peace desperately). I'm praying for so many things: that my boys would have as great a love for one another as a penchant for getting on one another's nerves; that God would direct and discipline their strengths and bless their proclivity for action while enabling restraint; that He would bring them to Himself so that they might love Him with their whole hearts and whole souls and whole minds; that God would shore up their weaknesses and prove Himself sufficient. I'm also praying that God would help my husband and me to model marriage and God's love for the church. And finally, I'm praying that God will open my eyes to see the answered prayer that is all around me.

Have you ever remarked to an acquaintance or a good friend that you'd pray for them or lift up a specific situation? And then have you forgotten? Or do you sometimes get so busy, so distracted, so *tired*, that you forget to pray for those things that are most important for your dearly loved ones? I have and I do. That's why words from Mark Batterson struck a chord: "The greatest tragedy in life is the prayers that go unanswered because they go unasked."[2] I have a responsibility to ask. And in some unfathomable way, my prayer can and does shift the course of world history.

I love sticky notes. I love to scatter them among legal materials I am reading to signify a particularly interesting or important point. I love to write lists on them. I jot down notes. To tell you the truth, there's something about just looking at a sticky note that makes the world seem a calmer, gentler place. Their appearance gives me a sense of order amidst chaos. And lately, in a very low-tech and simple way, I've started using them to remember to pray. I put sticky notes on the side of my computer screen, on my mirror, and even on my car's dashboard. They're a short and simple reminder to pray, a reminder that God hears and that, with Him, nothing is impossible.

Never, Ever Give Up

Walmart brings out the worst in my children. The large blue sign means one thing to my boys: toys! They start out bold. "Mom, can I have a remote-control truck?" Then they gradually moderate their requests. "What about a regular truck? A little one? Can we have a car? Okay, what about a tiny little car? You know the ones that are just ninety-seven cents?" Ah, the joys of Walmart.

But toddlers don't corner the market on persistent requests. Take, for example, Abraham's conversation with God in Genesis 18. The Lord was distressed at the wickedness of Sodom and Gomorrah— places where the poor, foreign, and disadvantaged were abused with impunity—and He planned to destroy the cities. Because Abraham's nephew Lot lived in Sodom, he asked the Lord to spare it. Can't you hear a toddler's voice in Abraham's persistent negotiation?

Abraham: "Will you indeed sweep away the righteous with the wicked? Suppose there are fifty righteous within the city" (verse 24–24).

The Lord: "If I find at Sodom fifty righteous in the city, I will spare the whole place for their sake" (verse 26).

Abraham: "Behold, I have undertaken to speak to the Lord, I who am but dust and ashes. Suppose five of the fifty righteous are lacking. Will you destroy the whole city for lack of five?" (verse 27).

The Lord: "I will not destroy it if I find forty-five there" (verse 28).

Abraham: "Suppose forty are found there."

The Lord: "For the sake of forty I will not do it" (verse 29).

Abraham: "Oh let not the Lord be angry, and I will speak. Suppose thirty are found there."

The Lord: "I will not do it, if I find thirty there" (verse 30).

Abraham: "Behold, I have undertaken to speak to the Lord. Suppose twenty are found there."

The Lord: "For the sake of twenty I will not destroy it" (verse 31).

Abraham: "Oh let not the Lord be angry, and I will speak again but this once. Suppose ten are found there."

The Lord: "For the sake of ten I will not destroy it" (verse 32).

Can you imagine? The temerity? The persistence? Abraham, concerned about his nephew and his family, asked the Lord to save an entire city on account of fifty people. But he didn't stop there. No less than *five* times did Abraham repeat his request: "What if there are fewer righteous people, Lord?" Abraham is refreshingly childlike in his requests. In response to God's gracious answers, Abraham becomes even bolder.

And God the Father responded. The Lord granted each of Abraham's increasingly outrageous requests. He did not get exasperated with Abraham—not once. As a Walmart-shopping parent, I find the Lord's patience incredible. I too easily forget that He has a Father's heart. And not just any Father's heart but a perfect Father's heart. I too easily forget that He, too, wants to give us good gifts. I forget that He wants to dialogue with us. Even though the Lord knows the desires of our hearts, He wants us to talk them over with Him. He wants a relationship with us.

Gifts are one of my husband's love languages, one he employs with joy and skill. He takes the time and thought to come up with just the right gift for an occasion. It's not unusual for him to come home from a trip with a special gift for our kids. As a result, our kids greet him at the door with demands for a "s'prise."

But recently Josh was as excited about giving the "s'prise" as the boys were about receiving it. Each received a law-enforcement badge with the insignia of the state of Missouri and my husband's name engraved across the top. For boys who "want to be police officers" when they grow up, the gifts could not have been more perfect. They were official! But it was my husband's joy that was complete. Seeing his delight in the boys' delight made me think about a God who longs to give us good gifts. My husband's expression at seeing two sets of joy-filled eyes gave life to Jesus' teaching that "it is more blessed to give than to receive" (Acts 20:35). As Luke puts it, "What father among you, if his son asks for a fish, will instead of a fish give him a serpent; or if he asks for an egg, will give him a scorpion?" (Luke 11:11-12).

The thought is incomprehensible. If, selfish as we are, we long to give good gifts to our children, how much more the perfect Father? God longs to give you good gifts.

Of course, sometimes the answer to prayer is no, or wait. Children instinctively know how to cope with the nos of life. Even though a no at Walmart may result in a rolling-on-the-floor tantrum, most kids get over the disappointment almost immediately. Their theatrics disguise an uncanny ability to persevere in the face of a negative answer. *No* doesn't harm children (quite the reverse; boundaries are instrumental in a child's development), nor does it squelch their desire for good things.

I remember walking through the store with my younger son, who had just turned two. He had an unhealthy fascination with candles. And we saw them everywhere. They were lurking around every aisle. Blaise demanded that we light some right then and there in the store. His mom, of course, said no. Blaise was distraught. Oh, the unfairness of the world! But within a few minutes of his heartfelt tantrum, he was back to his sunny self, cheerfully asking if we could purchase a football. (Um, no.) Children bounce back from no. They wait. They ask again.

In Luke 18, Jesus tells His disciples a story to show "that it was necessary for them to pray consistently and *never quit*" (Luke 18:1, MSG, emphasis mine). He told them about a certain widow in a certain town governed by a certain corrupt judge. The widow of Jesus' parable was in trouble. She asked for "justice" (verse 3). But the corrupt judge was entirely unconcerned with justice. He feared neither the Lord nor men. Yet the wicked judge eventually made things right because of the widow's persistence. She simply wore him down.

Jesus goes on to contrast the corrupt judge with the Righteous Judge: the God who is absolutely committed to bringing about justice, the God who cares for the widow and the orphan, the God who hears those crying out to Him day and night, the God who sees to justice, and quickly. This judge is a judge to whom we should pray always "and not lose heart" (Luke 18:1).

So, dear ones, if you're in a waiting season don't be discouraged. The Bible encourages us to be patient, as a farmer waiting for a crop. We can be patient and stand firm because we know the Lord is good, and that like a good parent, He longs to give us good gifts. In every season, no matter how difficult, He promises to be sufficient.

SIMPLE PRAYERS

I was once part of a Bible study that could have been put together only by the love of the King Most High. We were a diverse group—new Christians, old Christians, Catholic backgrounds, evangelical backgrounds, liberal, conservative, you name it. Regardless, every member of our new group, when I asked who wanted to close our study time in prayer, sat farther back in their chairs. Some of us hesitate to pray, especially with others, perhaps fearing we will get it wrong. Because prayer is so important, it seems as if there could be a right way and a wrong way to go about it.

But children show us that there's no wrong way to talk to God. Our kids teach us that prayer doesn't need to be fussy. Nor does it need to be eloquent. We don't pick up our kids from the sidewalk and kiss their skinned knees because they ask with a full sentence. We don't hold them close and comfort them when they are sick because they use proper grammar. We don't say yes to their heartfelt requests to read certain books because they phrase the query in perfect English. We answer because we love.

How much more will the Lord answer us because of His love, regardless of how awkwardly we may phrase a request? He desires your honest words. He wants to converse with you. He wants to hear your thoughts and feelings, your concerns and questions, your praises and your petitions. He wants a relationship with you—and that means talking to Him.

When we think about Jesus' teaching that we must become like a small child to enter the Kingdom, we realize that God the Father wants to hear our hearts, not particular phrases. There is no entrance exam other than the name of Jesus Christ. Indeed, one of the most effective prayers in the Bible and in everyday life is simply "Help me, Lord."

I love how James Montgomery describes the all-encompassing nature of prayer in his popular hymn.

Prayer is the soul's sincere desire
unuttered or expressed,
the motion of a hidden fire
that trembles in the breast.

Prayer is the burden of a sigh,
the falling of a tear,
the upward glancing of an eye,
when none but God is near.

Prayer is the simplest form of speech
that infant lips can try;
prayer the sublimest strains that reach
the Majesty on high.[3]

Montgomery concludes his hymn with "Lord, teach us how to pray."

Father God, as we watch our children ask for the outrageous time and time again, give us the boldness and simplicity to do the same. May we know that You hear us and answer us, however plain or grand our request. Lord, please grant us the tenacity to never, ever give up. Thank You, Lord Jesus.

Reflection Questions on Bold Requests

1. If you're hesitant to ask the Lord for a desire of your heart, ask yourself why that is. Does it seem too big, too outrageous? What is too big for God? Or does the desire seem too small, too insignificant? What could be too small for God to see and care about?

2. Do you believe deep in your heart that the Lord hears and cares enough to respond to those who seek Him? Read Hebrews 11:6.

3. Are you ever tempted to give up on a prayer? How can the stories of the persistent widow and the earthly father who gives good gifts help you persevere?

8

Limitless Joy

I have told you these things, that My joy and delight
may be in you, and that your joy and gladness may be
of full measure and complete and overflowing.

—JOHN 15:11, AMPC

The joy spread across Blaise's face stopped me in my tracks. He was only one year old, and his body was simply too small to contain the fullness of the moment. He erupted in a hop-skip, skitter-skatter of little feet. The object of his delight: a whirling ceiling fan. Blaise is frequently overcome by gleeful squeals over the discovery of a new rock. Or his brother's new remote-control car. Or the sight of his mom coming to pick him up from Sunday school. Or the same ceiling fan.

Little children live in a world where joy is just around the corner. Where seeing a dog on the way to the grocery store, or finding a frog in the garden, or having a brother's attention may delight at any moment. Life is full, an adventure expected to charm at every bend.

A limitless capacity for joy is chief among the characteristics that make children of the kingdom. Our children experience freely the good and perfect gifts our heavenly Father gives.

They are continually surprised by joy. And in this they show us the Father's heart for ourselves: a deep, abiding—and occasionally explosive—joy.

In fact, "surprised by joy" is how C. S. Lewis described his conversion in the book of the same name. Lewis thought the Christian life would be dreadfully dull and so described himself as "the most dejected and reluctant convert in all of England."[1] And yet God had a different plan; instead of drudgery, Lewis was taken aback by the joy he found in the person of Jesus and in the life to which Jesus had called him.

The nonbelieving Lewis had it backwards. Joy is one of the fruits of God's indwelling Spirit. Paul urges us to "rejoice in the Lord always" (Philippians 4:4). And theologian Gordon Fee explains that "unmitigated, untrammeled joy is—or at least should be—the distinctive mark of the believer in Jesus Christ."[2]

Does unmitigated, untrammeled joy characterize me? Is joy my distinctive mark? As I observe my children, I wonder why my heart hesitates to be this joyful, to dance in the streets like David, to expect good. Why do I despise the simple wonders of life as I pursue the substitutes for God that will never satisfy? In my struggle to be more, to control more, I too often lose out on the here and now. I too often lose out on the person of Jesus Christ.

Once again my children pull me back to Jesus. I know what unmitigated, untrammeled joy looks like because I see it in the face of my youngest child when he comes across a bouncy ball, a leftover Goldfish cracker in his car seat ("It's still good, Mama."), or that same ceiling fan. I see it in the face of my oldest boy when he snuggles close to man's best friend, when a wary cat finally lets the small boy near, and when he sounds out his first full book, *Mat Hid.*

Jesus invites us to experience at least these same levels of joy when we, like C. S. Lewis, encounter the risen Lord.

Joy through Relationship

"Mama, you're home!"

The spontaneous words of joy bring me to a standstill. My boys are at ages now when they enjoy spending the occasional afternoon with a babysitter. But they are still always overjoyed upon my return. "Mama, you're home!" reminds me of the childlike joy I can have in my relationship with Jesus. And the Bible tells us that God takes joy in His relationship with us too!

For most of my life, I've had a cramped view of God. I believed in Him. I knew that He sent His Son to die for my sins on a cursed cross. I knew that because of Him I might someday, somehow inherit eternal life. I was grateful and amazed. Yet truth be told, I wasn't sure that God cared much about day-to-day life. I distinctly remember sitting in the safety of a church pew as a child and wanting to stay there rather than return to the chaos of home. The stark juxtaposition of eternal happiness and everyday living was difficult to reconcile.

My view of the Lord is still much too small, but I understood the gospel in a new way when I realized that the Lord rescued us from sin and bondage *so that He might spend time with us and enjoy us*. Let me say that again: Jesus saved you not because He had to, not because it was His duty, but because He wanted to. The Cross was not some grudging act of sacrifice but a saving hand joyfully extended in friendship. As Psalm 18:16-19 tells us, God reached down from heaven to rescue us because He delights in us.

From time immemorial, God's grand plan has been to rescue humankind because He created us, values us, delights in us, and wants to enjoy us. His grand plan is to restore the garden fellowship, to walk among us, and through His Spirit to live in us.

The Old Testament tells the story well. Egypt represents the sin and slavery that entangle us all. And amazingly, the purpose of the Lord's great rescue of the Israelites from Egypt—from the sin and slavery and death that it represents—was so the Lord might have a relationship with His chosen people, the Israelites. He rescued them so He could dwell among them and be their God, so He could fellowship with them and call them His people. What a life-changing concept: The Lord reached down from heaven to save the Israelites because He wanted to enjoy them.

And all of this foreshadowed His great sacrifice of sending His only Son to die a ghastly death on the cross so we could stand in right relationship with Him. Jesus' ultimate sacrifice was meant to bring us back into relationship with God for the simple reason that God likes us and wants to spend time with us. As new parents exult in a baby, God delights in us and rejoices over us with singing.

This is all biblical. At the heart of the gospel message is the Lord's desire to be in close relationship with us, with you. He is the God who desires you, and He is the God who pursues you. As Zephaniah 3:17 tells us,

> The LORD your God is in your midst,
> a mighty one who will save;
> he will rejoice over you with gladness;
> he will quiet you by his love;
> he will exult over you with loud singing.

Hebrews tells us, in a shockingly stark way, that we are the reason Jesus endured the cross. We are urged to finish the race of life well as we "[fix] our eyes on Jesus, the author and perfecter of faith, *who for the joy set before Him endured the cross, despising the shame,* and has sat down at the right hand of the throne of God" (Hebrews 12:2, NASB, emphasis mine).

Let's sit with that truth. You were the joy set before Jesus as He endured the cross. He suffered the worst death that Rome had to offer, becoming a curse, so that you might live. Jesus came to save. He came to set prisoners free, to mend the brokenhearted, to bind the wounds. He came so that you might look to Him and live. And when push came to shove, and He had the choice of getting down off of the cross and making every Roman knee bow, He chose instead to endure its pain and shame *because Jesus saw you.* He longed for the day that you would believe in His name and be set free. He rejoiced over who you are and looked forward to the time when you would call Him Savior, Counselor, Lord, and Friend.

The joy of having a relationship with you, the joy of seeing you set free from the penalty and presence of sin and of knowing you in ever-increasing ways until you meet face-to-face, kept Him in place on the cross. As John Piper puts it, "His joy is in *our* redemption, which redounds to *God's* glory."[3] And it is that realization, that knowledge that He delights in you, which gives a whole new meaning to the gospel. You *are* the joy of the Lord.

JOY IN THE WORD

My children recently discovered *the* underpants books. There are a great many of them. Pirates, apparently, love underpants. So do dinosaurs and monsters. Aliens even use their stretchy fabric to save the earth from certain disaster in the form of an incoming meteor.

Now, when my kids decide they like a book, they *like* a book. It's the book of choice for days on end. It's the book chosen regardless of time of day. It's the book chosen above all other proffered options. It is *the* book. With this particular series, my boys particularly love the pictures. They admire, point, and giggle over the drawings of polka-dot, striped, solid, fancy, squeaky, or goopy underpants. They turn the book this way and that to get the best view. They obsess over the varieties. They meditate on the many uses. They delight in stories of daring rescues. There's no question; my kids take joy in reading about underpants.

As I watch their antics, I desire to have their joy in reading *the Book*. We are instructed to delight in, meditate on, and store up God's Word in our hearts. We are even called to consume those words. *Eat This Book* is the provocative title of Eugene Peterson's book about reading the Bible. We should read Scripture formatively, Peterson writes, in order to live. This is not a new idea. Jeremiah "ate" the books of the law, and they "became for [him] a joy and the delight of [his] heart" (Jeremiah 15:16, NASB). Ezekiel, too, devours the word of God: "Then I ate it, and it was as sweet as honey in my mouth" (Ezekiel 3:3, AMPC). And Jesus reminded the disciples that "[people] shall not live by bread alone, but by every word that comes from the mouth of God" (Matthew 4:4). Yet it's easy for me to forget that reading and meditating on God's Word is as necessary as the daily task of eating.

God longs to speak to you today. And the primary way He does so is through the Bible. In the Bible, we see Christ revealed.

We glimpse the story of creation, fall, and redemption and begin to understand our unique place in that story. We meet Grace Himself and learn that all of our sins have been forgiven. We begin to internalize the truths that we are adored daughters of the King of kings and that we are never alone.

The longest psalm in the Bible, Psalm 119, is all about reading God's Word with delight. The author obsesses over Scripture with an intensity that rivals my kids' affinity for the underpants books. He treasures it, rejoices in it, meditates on it, delights in it, and even pants (no pun intended) for it. He knows it, sings it, prays it, and acknowledges its worth.

Now listen, moms of littles, there is no condemnation here. I am right where you are, with good intentions but nothing from which to draw. My plans to get up early evaporate with the sixth waking during the night. I know how difficult a morning quiet time is when children wake early and often. And in this, as in all things, the Lord "upholds all who are falling and raises up all who are bowed down" (Psalm 145:14).

Moms, Jesus *knows* your heart; He knows exhaustion that goes bone deep, the kind of tired that, as an acquaintance recently remarked, makes your face literally hurt. Yet, or perhaps because of this, Jesus went away as often as possible to hear from His Father God.

My kids' obsession with underpants has me wondering what I can learn. What if I obsessed over God's Word in the same manner? What if, instead of measuring my quiet time by my pre-kid standards, I took a few verses, a psalm, or even one verse and read *to live*? What if I ruminated upon that Scripture all day? What if I turned the passage over and over again in my mind as I fed the kiddos, drove them to school, picked up toys, managed a work deadline, and put the boys to bed at night? What if I incorporated the verse into my prayers? What if I read Scripture formatively, expecting it to transform me? In this season, one verse may be all a mom like me can manage some days, but that verse has the power to change. It's living, God-breathed Scripture appointed just for me today.

May we find His words today and devour them. May Scripture be the delight of our hearts. May we pray, paraphrasing the author of Psalm 119: *Lord, incline our hearts to Your word. Open our eyes that we may behold wonderful things in Your law. May the unfolding of Your words give light. And may our understanding be made fuller, richer, and deeper in the knowledge of who You are.*

Joy from Forgiveness

The other night Elijah asked me a funny question as I was putting him to bed. "Mama, are boys smarter than girls?"

I was surprised by the question and responded, "No, honey. What makes you ask that?"

"Well," Elijah explained, "You're wrong all the time, and Daddy never is."

I laughed out loud and assured my son that, yes, Daddy is sometimes wrong. But thinking on his question today not only makes me laugh, it gives me joy because I'm slowly discovering a new freedom in being wrong. As someone who has spent a lot of years trying to gain acceptance through performance, I'm realizing it's okay to accept my imperfections, because Jesus came to set all things right. I'm grateful that Elijah knows I often make mistakes, and I'm praying he learns that it's okay when he makes mistakes as well. For it's when we mess up that we experience the loving-kindness of a God who forgives us completely and who loves us with a perfect Father's heart.

Despite our earthly circumstances, God's children can have joy because we are a forgiven people. When we say yes to Jesus, our sins are forgiven! We are automatically in a right relationship with God because of Jesus' substitutionary payment for our sins.

Let's consider an amazing thing that happened when Jesus defeated sin and made it possible for us to receive God's forgiveness. The Temple veil was split in two. This veil was no ordinary curtain. Historians estimate that it was sixty feet high and three to four inches thick. It separated the place of God's dwelling—the Holy of Holies—from the rest of the Temple. The high priest was the only person allowed to enter this sacred place, and he only once a year. The Temple veil was a tangible sign of the impassible, sin-created gulf between God and man.

That all changed in an instant. The moment Christ died the Temple veil was torn in two. The chasm between God and man was bridged. Through Jesus, we may freely approach the very throne room of God, something unheard of in Old Testament times. We have nothing to fear because, when the Lord looks at us, He sees the righteousness of Jesus. In Christ, we are forgiven all. As Lisa Bevere says, "When I look to myself, I see flaws; when I look to Christ, my imperfections are lost in his radiance."[4]

Yet for some reason it isn't always easy for us to accept God's forgiveness. And it isn't always easy for us to offer forgiveness to others either. And that's when we miss the joy God wants us to have. If we want to see the joy of forgiveness, our children offer a good example. They show us how to live in and to accept the unwarranted forgiveness of God.

❧

Elijah *loves* a project. It had been a cold, windy winter week. So we were forced to improvise. We planted a small garden in a few old pots (this involved fitting as many seeds as possible into as close a space as possible and then dousing them with about a gallon of water) and waited for a miracle. And come, it did—though the event of germination was quite unexpected and miraculous. Spring pea shoots poked up through the soil. A lonely, sole-surviving squash seed—the other seeds' typical hardiness no match for my four-year-old—began pushing leaves through saturated soil. And a few brave marigolds dared peek their heads above the surface.

Elijah was overjoyed. His garden was a splendid success, and he enjoyed watching it and watering it. One morning as we were having breakfast, he asked to see the garden. He was admiring the fast-growing squash plant in particular. That particular plant also managed to pique the dangerous interest of his younger brother. I was busy putting breakfast away when Elijah squawked, "Mom, Blaise is looking at my plant."

I naively replied, "It's *okay* Elijah; he won't hurt it."

Famous last words.

Out of the corner of my eye, I saw a glint in Blaise's eyes. With one firm and victorious tug, he pulled the squash plant up by its roots. Elijah lost his cool. Once the wailing diminished to the decibel level of an airplane hangar, Blaise apologized (I'm not sure his "sowwy" was sincere and suspect he'd yank Mr. Squash out by the roots again given the chance). Apology in hand, we stuffed the squash back into the container (he's still alive today, though decidedly yellow).

I swept up the soil-covered floor and looked up in amazement as sounds of little-boy laughter filled the kitchen. Both boys were wreathed in smiles, co-collaborators in breaking a sacred table rule: Do not throw food. One would throw a piece and the other would laugh uproariously. Then it was the other one's turn. The sheer contrast between the back-to-back scenes left me unable to discipline the food-throwing rascals. Where there had been anger and outrage (justified in fact if not in degree), there was now camaraderie. Elijah had fully and completely forgiven his younger brother and brought Blaise back into relationship. There was not a hint of leftover bitterness, just joy in having an ornery younger brother. Their antics remind me to let go of my own bitterness, to forgive, and when it's too difficult, to ask the Lord to help me to do so.

Even more, I wonder at Blaise's complete lack of embarrassment or shame. He accepted forgiveness with two chubby, open hands and he never looked back. He allowed himself to be fully restored to relationship. He did not bludgeon himself with his failure. For the millionth time I wonder who is teaching whom. Jesus offers us just this sort of all-encompassing forgiveness, a forgiveness from which we can move on without shame or embarrassment.

It can be so easy to hold on to our sin, to let past regrets hinder future obedience, to feel worthless and unlovable because of something we have done or failed to do. But our children show us how to accept God's forgiveness. Just think: Our most regrettable moments are remembered no longer, washed away by the blood flowing red from our Savior. The Lord has removed our transgressions from us as far as the east is from the west. Once we repent and ask forgiveness, the Lord sees only righteousness. It is grace. It is Jesus.

Joy in Hope

The boys were plastered to the windows as we took the break-of-dawn plane ride to Colorado. Their dad had told them about the surprise village we were visiting. A village that—like the Mickey Mouse clubhouse—appeared out of thin air when one spoke the password. A village revealed only to those who knew the secret. A mystical village beyond their wildest imagination.

Their anticipation was palpable. And even the long plane ride followed by the even longer car ride did not dim their excitement. Around every bend, over every mountain peak, came the urgent questions and comments.

"Are we there?"

"Can we say the password now?"

"I think this is it!"

They waited, all bated breath and breathless wonder. And then, finally, their dad said it was time, the boys spoke the password, and the small mountain village of Vail, Colorado, was revealed. Shrieks of joy filled the car. Interestingly, it wasn't just the moment of discovery that was joy filled, or the vacation itself, but the entire (long!) journey. The boys' anticipation extended their joy beyond the moment of fulfillment. Their anticipation of a future hope led to happy shivers of anticipation and a bliss-filled, expectant journey.

As I think this morning about our summer vacation, I hear the Lord's gentle whisper: "Do you treat this life you're living as the precursor to the ultimate gift—eternity with me? Do you shiver with anticipation knowing that each bend in the road, every season, good and bad, every moment, brings you one step closer to me? Dear one, I'm waiting with bated breath to have you with me always. I'm waiting to wipe away every tear. I'm waiting to rejoice over you. I cannot wait to be with you and to share a cup of coffee. Are you looking forward to being with me?"

As Jesus called the little children to Him, as they leapt and bounded into His arms with exuberant unselfconsciousness, as they ran to Him with joy, He likely saw in them the sort of anticipation He wants to see in me. Our children's capacity for anticipation not only increases their enjoyment but provides fuel and perseverance for their hope.

Anticipation takes up hope and makes it come alive. It considers hope, turns it over, and examines it from all sides. Anticipation includes feelings of excitement, enthusiasm, eagerness, and pre-fulfillment joy.[5] It's thumping hearts, eager hands, feet dancing up and down, hands-over-mouth excitement. Anticipation is Christmas Eve.

The science of psychology tells us that anticipation increases joy before, during, and after a looked-forward-to event.[6] My children's pre-arrival vacation excitement bears this out. As it did for my children waiting for the hidden village, joyful anticipation makes hope real and tangible.

The apostle Paul knew the power of anticipatory hope. Paul was well acquainted with trial and tragedy. He was stoned once, beaten with a rod three times, and given thirty-nine lashes five times. He faced death again and again on his travels and was thrice shipwrecked. He was hungry, thirsty, and cold. Like a new mom, Paul worked long and hard, enduring numerous sleepless nights. Like a new mom, he worried daily about those committed to his care.

In the midst of all these circumstances, Paul could be joyfully content because he anticipated eternity with Jesus. He "rejoic[ed] in hope of the glory of God" (Romans 5:2). The original Greek word *kauchomai* means to glory, rejoice, or boast "from a particular vantage point."[7] Paul was rejoicing in anticipatory hope from the vantage point of someone who had already experienced God's promises and therefore has utmost confidence in them.

Interestingly, the root word for boast, *kaux*, is always written in the Greek middle voice. The middle voice—something missing from the English language—indicates that the subject of the verb is acting upon himself or for his own benefit. Thus, Paul's boasting in the Lord benefitted Paul. He was encouraged and emboldened as he rejoiced in the glory of God.

Paul, in other words, was a joyful anticipator. He knew that his present troubles—as real as prison walls—paled in comparison to the glory waiting for him. Paul's boasting in the hope of the glory of God is a lot like my children's vacation anticipation. This future hope encouraged Paul in the midst of trials. The journey was one of anticipation. Dear ones, we too can use the Greek middle voice to encourage ourselves in trying circumstances. We can anticipate God's promises in the midst of piles of laundry and during those difficult-to-discipline days—and we too can hope as ones who have already seen the Lord acting in our lives.

The Bible encourages us to live in a constant state of anticipation. We are the bride, beautifully adorned with the righteousness of Christ, who awaits her bridegroom, Christ Himself. Regardless of our circumstances, we can joyfully hope in the promise of eternal life with Jesus. We can, quite simply, look forward to being with Him.

Similarly, and also regardless of our circumstances, we can joyfully hope in the work God is doing in us and for us here on earth. As Philippians 1:6 promises, He who "began a good work in you will bring it to completion at the day of Jesus Christ." Dear friend, what are you expecting the Lord to do today? Tomorrow?

If you've misplaced that keen childhood sense of anticipation, you are not alone. A. W. Tozer writes that "one characteristic that marks the average church today is lack of anticipation. Christians, when they meet, do not expect anything unusual to happen."[8]

The church's lack of anticipation is not a new phenomenon. In Acts 12, we read of Peter's miraculous escape from prison and of his friends who expected nothing out of the ordinary. To set the scene: Herod had just killed James, the brother of Jesus. Herod had also arrested Peter, and the church gathered at Mary's home to pray for his release from prison. But they didn't expect him literally to show up at the door. And for good reason. Peter was bound in chains, sleeping between two soldiers in a heavily guarded prison.

Yet that is precisely what happened. An angel loosed Peter's chains and walked him through sleeping guards. Peter went directly to Mary's house and knocked on the outer door. The maid recognized his voice but in her excitement left Peter standing outside as she ran back into the house shouting, "Peter is at the door." And the very people who were gathered to pray for Peter's release refused to believe it was him. Surely it must be an angel, they said. Peter kept on knocking, and when they finally opened the door, they were astonished.

The disciples once again remind us of our own tendency to

doubt. It's easy to fail to expect the unexpected, to overlook the miraculous. It's easy to forget that the present and momentary afflictions we face will become inconsequential when we meet Jesus face-to-face. It's easy to forget to boast in the hope of the future glory of God.

My boys are a living parable showing me the importance of joyful anticipation. They are *always* on the lookout for something unusual to happen—and this expectation is more often than not manifested in reality. Because they are looking for it, simple moments become wondrous. A vacation village. A fish jumping out of the water. A sunrise or sunset. The crescent moon. A new baby. The Lord's presence and caretaking made manifest. As Tozer concludes, "We must declare war on the mood of nonexpectation, and come together with childlike faith. Only then can we know again the beauty and wonder of the Lord's presence among us."[9]

Joy in the Interruptions

Children show us the blessing of living in the margins, of wasting time. As we grow up, we learn to multitask and prioritize; we become agenda driven. Even when home with my littles, I have this insatiable desire to check off activities and accomplishments at day's end and to seek fulfillment in a productive day. But toddlers upend the best-laid plans. They take joy in the interruptions.

The other day, for example, I had a rather fabulous idea: Why not catch tadpoles at our neighbor's nearby pond? It would be fun *and* educational. We would watch them grow legs, lose their tails, and morph into frogs. The plan: Scooter up the driveway, walk along the path, have fun catching tadpoles. The reality: Scooter up the driveway, scooter back down the driveway as fast as possible. Repeat. Repeat again. And again. Start walking along the path. Pick wildflowers for Mom. Repeat with each new weed, *ahem*, flower. Continue walking along the path. Find a shivering baby bunny while looking for weed-flowers. Watch baby bunny. Watch baby bunny some more. Baby bunny finally hops off. Continue on path. Jump off an old hay bale. Repeat. Repeat again. Arrive at the pond. Stop to look at minnows. Try to catch said minnows. "Accidently" step into pond and soak shoes. Meander along pond's edge as slowly as possible. Find tadpoles. Realize that we are too exhausted to catch tadpoles.

The days I can let go of best-laid plans and live in the moment of unhurried enjoyment are the days when baby bunnies surprise and sunlight glistens on the pond. I am slowly learning (and relearning) that life is lived in the interruptions. Henri Nouwen tells the story of an old Notre Dame professor who looked back on his long teaching career and remarked, "I have always been complaining that my work was constantly interrupted, until I slowly discovered that my interruptions were my work."[10] For me, the story is more poignant because Professor Nouwen is talking about himself. The illustrious biblical scholar found his God-given work manifested most often not in his next book or lecture but in those pesky interruptions.

Children relish interruptions. They live where curiosity sparkles and life happens. They are delighted with each new unfolding event and wholly unworried about "the plan." In fact, in interruptions, children see *the plan*. They demonstrate Jesus' heart by showing us that it is the journey that teaches, that encourages, that speaks life, and that sanctifies. After all, the final battle has already been won.

When Jesus called the little children to Himself, when He snuggled them close, joy was a characteristic that likely stood out to Him. Joy is the distinctive mark of children. They overflow with simple joy at our mere presence. They enjoy reading with their moms. They happily accept full forgiveness for their transgressions. They are ecstatic as they anticipate Christmas Eve and delight in the interruptions of life. Dear ones, Jesus wants you to have a childlike joy in Him today. He wants you to overflow with joy.

Reflection Questions on Limitless Joy

1. Is joy your distinctive mark? If not, why not? Are there promises of God that you struggle to fully believe?

2. Do you believe that God sent His Son to save you because He delights in you? Because He wants to spend time with you? Meditate on this truth by reading Psalm 18:16, Zephaniah 3:17, and Hebrews 12:2.

3. Do you read the Bible to live? If not, what is one thing you can do in the midst of the busyness to focus on a single verse during your day? Ask God to bring Scripture to mind as you go about your day and to be present with you in the busyness.

4. Is there anything from your past that's holding you back from living the life to which the Lord has called you? Ask the Lord to help you believe that you are the righteousness of Christ, that your sins are as far from you as east from west—that you are forgiven.

5. What would it look like to live with more childlike anticipation—to live like it's Christmas Eve? How would this sort of anticipation change how you go about your day?

9

Lean Up

*One thing have I asked of the L*ORD*, that will I seek
after: that I may dwell in the house of the L*ORD
*all the days of my life, to gaze on the beauty
of the L*ORD *and to inquire in his temple.*

—PSALM 27:4

I n a recent interview, Sheryl Sandberg, the amazingly successful Facebook COO, one of the youngest female billionaires, and
popular and influential women's author of *Lean In*, noted that she
has an uncomfortable relationship with power, ambition, and lead-
ership.[1] She has money, a fulfilling job, and an influential voice. Yet
she wrote in *Lean In*, "I still have days when I feel like a fraud."[2] In
other words, she may still have the nagging feeling that she is not
enough.

And the truth is that she is not because we are not. We are not
enough when we lean in and pursue our goals with gusto, as good
as that principle is. We are not enough when we work harder or
when we work smarter. Quite simply, we are enough only because
Jesus is enough. We are enough only when we *lean up*—when we
rely on Jesus and desire a relationship with Him above all else. We

are enough when Jesus is our guiding light, our strength, and our home. We are enough when the one thing we truly desire is to sit in His courts.

Children instinctively know that they are not enough. One day I was watching VeggieTales' *Noah's Ark* with Elijah. He sat rapt as the unfortunate guinea pig that had been the subject of Shem's many flying experiments was reunited at long last with his mate. A joyful reunion ensued, and my three-year-old, assuming the reunion was between mother and son, exclaimed, "He found his mommy!"

What a privilege and responsibility to be the center of someone's life. How humbling to be the one they would most like to find. I know it's fleeting, but for the moment my toddler's life revolves around his parents. This will change. Friends, girlfriends, someday a wife, and most importantly, Jesus (we pray) will occupy that space in his heart. But for me now, it's a humbling picture of relational value. My son just wants to be with me.

When Jesus speaks of becoming childlike, one thing He must have in mind is children's desire to be with their mom and dad. As a wise mom once said, "A mom *is* home." Very young children especially illustrate this principle. Because they do not yet understand that objects continue to exist even though they cannot be observed (object permanence), little ones want to keep their moms especially close.

As I think about being childlike, I wonder whether I desire this sort of intimacy with Jesus. Is Jesus the one I would most like to find? Does my life revolve around Him, my Rock and my Redeemer? Would I leap over a classroom table if Jesus were to pick me up from Sunday school? Is Jesus *home*?

LEANING UP INTO RELATIONSHIP

Luke 10 reminds us that only *one* thing is required. In that relatable example, Jesus surprises His friends Mary and Martha with a visit. Can you imagine? The honor, the excitement, the privilege of hosting Jesus? And then the worry. Dinner is rather pedestrian, the sink is piled high with dirty dishes, and the children's toys are strewn about the living room. It would be so easy to be Martha—to be distracted by, as Luke puts it, "much serving" (Luke 10:40).

Mary, in contrast, drops everything to sit at the Lord's feet. Her first priority is to be with Jesus. Listening to Him matters more to her than doing good work or appearances. Her primary desire is to be with Jesus and to soak up His presence and His words. Like a small child, she sits at His feet, content simply to be there with Him. When Martha complains, Jesus tells her that Mary's desire to lean up into relationship is the better part.

Jesus wants *us*, not our service. According to Jesus, the most important command is not to do more or to be more but to love Him more. He says in Luke 10:27, you must "love the Lord your God with all your heart and with all your soul and with all your strength and with all your mind." Children give us a picture of such love in action. They simply want to be with their moms.

In Exodus 33:7-11, we're told the story of Joshua. A young aide, Joshua would help Moses as he worshipped the Lord in the tent of meeting. There the Lord would speak to Moses as to a friend. And then Moses would leave to continue his work of leading the Israelite nation. But the Bible tells us that Joshua chose to stay. After every time of worship, Joshua refused to leave the Lord's presence.

He would remain in the tent alone. As the aide to the leader of an enormous and displaced nation, there's little doubt that Joshua had other duties. But there he sat. He remained in the Lord's presence: He leaned up. Joshua desired most to be with God the Father, just as small children want to be with their parents.

When Blaise was small, he caught the norovirus, otherwise known as the winter vomiting bug. This particular bug comes complete with a fever, aches, diarrhea, and intense vomiting. Blaise could not have been more miserable. He had finally fallen asleep snuggled in beside me and was burning up. Thinking that my body heat was making him even warmer, I tried to extricate myself. Blaise was having none of it. With a frantic cry, he turned his burning face to mine and snuggled deeper. In the midst of his fever, the only balm for his soul was intimate closeness. Blaise was desperate to lean up.

What about us? When we're burning up with fever which way do we lean? When we are burning up with tiredness, misplaced dreams, empty promises, and the ultimate realization that we are not enough, which way do we lean? Do we grasp for the hem of Jesus' cloak, or do we turn away? Do we redouble our own efforts, or do we lean up? Are we absolutely *desperate* to snuggle close?

The Father's arms are waiting. The Bible tells us over and over again that Jesus, the King of kings, turned His attention to those who were hurting most. To the widow, to the childless, to the woman who had been bleeding for twelve years, to outcast tax collectors, and even to sinners like the woman at the well, Jesus entered into their worst and gave them His best.

The key: Instead of going it on their own, they leaned up, seeking and finding Jesus. When we are burning up, there's only one thing to do. Lean up. Go and sit at the feet of Jesus. Ask the hard questions. Tell Him about your heartache, and let Him pour living water over you. He is the King who makes beauty from ashes. He is the one who breathes Spirit-life, making the dry bones of past dreams live and breathe and dance.

For now, my sons' lives are ordered around my husband and me. We are the constants in a world that must at times seem overwhelming. We are the ones who can (sometimes) institute order, the ones who make sense out of a scary world. We are the ones who protect and who have their interests at heart. We are the ones who love unconditionally (though imperfectly).

As my boys lean up, I tremble at the responsibility, but I am grateful for the metaphor. When we desire Christ like our children desire us, our lives become ordered around Him. He is not one of many things but *the* thing. It is in Him that we find our life and our all and our purpose. When we, like small children with their parents, desire to be with Jesus most, He becomes our constant. In a world that is riddled with sin-brokenness, Jesus is Lord. And He loves us. There is nothing to do but lean up.

Leaning Up into Promises

My four-year-old is potty-trained—sort of. He dislikes going number two, which of course turns out to be an unfortunate, nearly daily necessity. He waits and waits and waits. Accordingly, I have resorted to a reward system: a single, enormous marshmallow. Recently, Elijah used the restroom at the grocery store, and by the time we got home, his marshmallow had been forgotten. Until the middle of the night, that is, when he awoke with a desperate sense of injustice; he had not received his due reward. And he needed it *now.* Elijah's antics remind me that children have the memory of an elephant, at least when it comes to a reward/bribe. They never forget a promise, especially one that involves marshmallows.

Yet how often do we forget, or at least forget to internalize, the glorious promises that the Lord has made to us? Let's remind ourselves of a few:

- He will be with us.
- He will never fail us or forsake us.
- The poor and oppressed will see justice.
- Deep waters will not overwhelm and though we pass through fire we will not be burned.
- We need not fear nor be dismayed because He will uphold and strengthen us.
- He loves us and calls us His own.
- He will rescue us.
- His covenant is an everlasting one.
- He has our best interests at heart.
- He knows everything about us—and adores us still.

Children lean up because they arc loved. So are we. The verse is familiar, but the promise of eternal life is worth repeating: "This is how much God loved the world: He gave his Son, his one and only Son. And this is why: so that no one need be destroyed; by believing in him, anyone can have a whole and lasting life" (John 3:16, MSG). God loved us so much that He willingly sent His only Son, His beloved Son, to die a criminal's death on an instrument of Roman torture. And Jesus loved us so much that He willingly endured the cross.

Like my then four-year-old, I don't want to forget the important promises. I want to claim the promises of God. Daily. I want to walk in them, to be free in them, to find light and life in them. I want to lean up into the promises that I am loved beyond measure, that God is my strength and my shield, and that He is with me wherever I go. As I lean up to the Lord like a small child, His promises and not the cacophony of the world's voices become my confidence.

LEANING UP INTO HIS PRESENCE

When the Lord chose the Israelites as *His* people, the people through whom He was going to bless the entire world, He made them unique. He set them apart. He didn't use conventional means to do so, however. He didn't provide them with a new language, a special handshake, or a distinctive uniform. Instead, the Lord set apart the Israelites by giving them Himself. He promised to be with them. He promised to go before them through the wilderness as a pillar of fire by night and a cloud by day. He was a banner of love over them, protecting and encouraging them.

The Israelites understood *the* thing that made them unique was the Lord's presence. In fact, the circumstance that Moses feared the most—more than the armies of Pharaoh, marauding nations, or the harshness of the wilderness—was the Lord's absence. Modeling our own inclination to fall away, the Israelites soon forgot their spectacular rescue from Egyptian slavery, the Lord's miraculous parting of the Red Sea, and His provision in the wilderness. They made (of all things) a golden calf to worship. The Lord was not pleased and threatened to remove His presence from Israel. Moses was aghast because he knew that the single defining attribute of Israel was that they were God's chosen people. Their sole distinguishing characteristic was the Lord's presence. So Moses pleaded with the Lord:

> If your presence will not go with me, do not bring us up from here. For how shall it be known that I have found favor in your sight, I and your people? Is it not in your going with us, so that we are distinct, I and your people, from every other people on the face of the earth? Exodus 33:15-16

The Lord relented. "This very thing that you have spoken I will do," the Lord replied, "for you have found favor in my sight, and I know you by name" (Exodus 33:17).

As believers, we are heirs to the Israelites' uniqueness. He is pleased with us and *He knows our name*. God chooses us and delights in us. We are also successors to God's covenantal promises. We know that He will never leave or forsake us. We know that Jesus has once and for all set us free from the penalty of sin. We know the Lord set us aside for His purposes—so that through us, somehow, the world might be blessed. Astonishingly, as New Testament believers, we are in an even better position than God's chosen people. The old pillar of fire has been replaced by a new and incredible gift: the indwelling Holy Spirit.

I'm reminded of a particularly rough day when my two-and-a-half-year-old didn't seem to respond to discipline. I hated seeing tears in his eyes, and I felt overwhelmed at the task of helping him learn to control his pendulum of emotions. Then, Francesca Battistelli's song "Holy Spirit" came on the radio. The chorus, which asks God to flood the place with His presence, stopped my thoughts in their tracks.

We sang a version of this song at my old church in Washington, DC, and my heart warmed with memories of welcoming the Lord to come and grace corporate worship, of singing in unison and seeking the presence of the Lord. But on this particular day, there was a different lesson for me.

"Ask for my presence not just at church, not just during the worship songs, but in the midst of the messiness of today," I heard the Lord whisper. *"Ask for my presence in the daily grind of diapers, spit-up, and tantrums. Seek my face when you have no idea how to discipline or what to do. Ask me to come flood every crevice of your home with the light of my love and grace. Ask me to fill the very atmosphere with my holy presence—every inch of it."*

You see, Jesus is ever so much bigger than church. We meet Him there, especially. But He is Word, and He is Truth, and He is Spirit. And He is with us now; the gift of His Holy Spirit is a constant.

For forty glorious days, the risen Jesus taught His disciples and revealed Himself to hundreds. He laughed with them and explained things to them. He restored Peter, shored up Thomas, and ate fish. Can you imagine the relentless joy that must have overwhelmed Jesus' followers? Their teacher and friend had been miraculously restored to them. And more than this, Jesus was who He said He was: the Son of God come into the world to defeat sin and death. The disciples finally understood the truth. Jesus was God and He had died for them. He was their everything. And they had been reunited with Him.

Now, can you imagine their horror when Jesus told the disciples that He must leave again? The disciples' hearts filled with sorrow. Yet Jesus reassured them, "Nevertheless, I tell you the truth: it is to your advantage that I go away, for if I do not go away, the Helper will not come to you. But if I go, I will send him to you" (John 16:7). Though difficult to understand, this passage tells us that somehow, incredibly, the disciples were in a better position after Jesus had ascended to heaven than when He was with them on earth.

I confess my mind rebels. Surely the disciples—surely we—would be better off were Jesus here to have and to hold. But while we wait for His return, we have the gift of the Holy Spirit—the gift Jesus insisted was better than His physical presence on earth. As Nicky Gumbel explains, "Jesus could only be in one place at a time. Now, by his Spirit, he can be with you and me as our friend and helper all the time, everywhere we go."[3]

A close look at the original Greek text sheds some light on the promised gift of the Holy Spirit. The word that Jesus used, *parakletos*, is translated different ways. The NIV translates it as Advocate, the ESV and the New King James as Helper, the King James and *Amplified Bible* (Classic Edition) as Comforter, and *The Message* as Friend. Each of these words gives us some sense of the promised gift of the Spirit. But as wonderful and apt as each of those terms is, it's really in combination that they help explain who the Holy Spirit is. The Spirit is our Advocate, Helper, Comforter, and Friend. And even then there is something lost in translation.

The Greek word *parakletos* is actually made up of two words: *para* and *kaleo.* Each gives us a deeper understanding of what Jesus meant when He described the Holy Spirit. *Para* means "from close beside" or "alongside." It emphasizes nearness and closeness; it implies "intimate participation." *Kaleo* means a legal advocate who makes the correct decision. Put the two together and you get an

Advocate who makes the correct decision *because He is intimately involved, because He is close alongside the person needing help.*

Jesus is thus talking about sending an Advocate, Helper, Comforter, Friend who will advocate for, help, and comfort us precisely because He is intimately involved in our lives. The Holy Spirit comes alongside of us, indwells us even, and advocates/helps/comforts/befriends us in just the right way because He is always near. The Holy Spirit reveals Christ and teaches us about Him. He hears our prayers and the groaning of our hearts and prays *for us.* The Holy Spirit knows us and pours out the love of God into our hearts. The Holy Spirit comforts us and gives us peace.

Now it's a little easier to see why Jesus told the disciples they were better off without Him—because His Spirit would indwell them, and us. We have the gift of His presence daily.

Our part is simple: Lean up. As believers, we need only to ask the Holy Spirit to come and flood our hearts and our homes, and He will fill the very atmosphere. We need only to ask Him to lead, guide, and protect us. We need only to welcome Him as children and to accept the love that Jesus longs to shed in our hearts. Make no mistake, the Advocate, Helper, Comforter, and Friend will come alongside of us. The funny thing is, when we invite Him into our messy lives, we discover that He is already there, waiting for us to lean up.

Dear ones, as we watch our young children snuggle up to us, let's remember what it means to lean up into relationship with Jesus. And as we go about our day-to-day tasks of caring for our children—and providing what we've promised them—let's call to mind the Lord's marvelous promises of full and abundant life here on earth and eternal life with Him in heaven. And finally, as small children bask in their parents' presence, let's delight in the very presence of God—His Holy Spirit, the Advocate and Comforter who comes alongside of us in just the way we need.

Reflection Questions on Lean Up

1. Can you remember a moment when you desperately needed the Lord? What did you do?

2. Which promises of God are particularly meaningful to you today? How can you remind yourself of them?

3. What might happen if you let the Holy Spirit minister to you as Advocate, Helper, Comforter, and Friend, who comes alongside you because He loves you and knows you intimately?

10

Trust

[Most] blessed is the [wo]man who believes in,
trusts in, and relies on the Lord, and whose
hope and confidence the Lord is. For [s]he shall be
like a tree planted by the waters that spreads out its
roots by the river; and it shall not see and fear when
heat comes; but its leaf shall be green. [She] shall not
be anxious and full of care in the year of drought,
nor shall [she] cease yielding fruit.

—JEREMIAH 17:7-8, AMPC

The pool lay just beyond the wide kitchen window. We were visiting my husband's extended family, and I stood rooted in place, watching with the horror and disbelief of a new mom. An athletic lot, my husband's cousins were reenacting the Olympic diving competition. They'd run and flip face-first into the none-too-deep pool. Of course, the younger cousins wanted to join in the fun and were soon being tossed into the water. They'd emerge in smiling splutter-gasps and climb out for more. Then to my horror, an older cousin picked up Katie, the smallest girl, and did a front flip into the pool with her in his arms. Her mom quickly came out to forbid such future foolishness. But Katie's reaction was astounding. She loved it! She wasn't afraid because she trusted in the arms that held her close.

Here's a less dramatic but more common example: dads throwing their small children up in the air. For the watching mom, it's heart stopping. The little bundle you've protected with your literal body and every ounce of your sleep-deprived energy is now flying seven or eight feet up in the air. We've all heard the tales (laughingly told!) of dads throwing their kids up into the ceiling fan. Notwithstanding my motherly misgivings, my kids delight in being "tossed." They laugh, squeal, and hug their dad's legs, begging to be launched skyward. "Again! Again!" The thought that they might fall does not even cross their minds. They fully trust the arms that will catch them and so fly upward without fear.

As I watch my brave children, they teach me about trust. They understand what trust is: a leaning of one's whole weight upon another. They also instinctively know that when you lean your whole weight upon something, you relinquish your own grasp at control. For children, that's part of the fun! And a child's relationship to her parents shows us that much of Mom's and Dad's love goes unseen by the child. In the same way, our Father God is always at work on our behalf, even when His footprints are not clearly visible.

A Leaning Weight

Blaise had fallen fast asleep in our vehicle. Once we arrived home, I urged his older brother to be quiet, and we attempted the impossible: moving Blaise from car seat to waiting bed without waking the sleeping giant. On this particular day, Blaise was so deep in sleep that he never moved. He was relaxed, completely limp, and the entirety of his dead weight centered against my chest as I carried him up the stairs. This particular thirty-two pounds of toddler boy had never been so still. Heart to heart, his center of gravity rested heavy on me. With a pressure that evoked mama-bear feelings of love and protection, Blaise leaned his whole weight upon my body. There was not one fiber of his being that resisted the direction we were going or tried to strike off on its own.

The dead weight of Blaise on my chest reminds me of the story of John Paton, a nineteenth-century Scottish missionary to the New Hebrides islands. During that time period, the islands were not particularly hospitable to visitors. Only nineteen years before John Paton landed on the island of Tanna (with his wife), the first and only two missionaries to the New Hebrides had been *killed and eaten* by the islanders within minutes of stepping ashore.

Paton and his family were in constant danger. Nevertheless, they were determined to share the Good News. Paton learned the native language in order to translate the Gospel of John. He was surprised to find that the language contained no words for "faith," "belief," or "trust." These concepts were alien to a culture of constant fear.

Paton struggled to find a word to express trust. One day he had an idea: As described by author Nicky Gumbel, he leaned back in his chair, took both feet off the floor, and asked his indigenous housekeeper to describe his action.[1] The native replied with a word that meant "to lean your whole weight upon."[2] This word became the expression that Paton used for trust and faith—an expression that meant to lean one's whole weight upon Jesus.

I love this description of trust—the ability to lean back, let all tension and striving cease, and rest my entire weight on the King of kings. This sort of complete abandon is the trust I see in my children as they fly into the air (or heaven forbid, front flip into a pool). Jesus invites us to trust Him fully. To lean our whole weight upon Him, knowing that He will catch us. As 1 Peter 5:7 tells us, we can cast *all* of our cares, our entire weight, upon Jesus—holding nothing back—because He cares for us.

It is when we have this leaning-weight sort of trust that we can live within the meaning of the Old Testament term *shalom*. Shalom means peace, but also much more. It's a state of well-being, of completeness and contentment. It's a place where fear and anxiety meet their ends in Jesus. It is, in the words of Isaiah 26:3, the "perfect peace" of those who trust in the Lord.

I am constantly amazed by photos of babies snuggled close to their moms in the worst of circumstances, sleeping contently as air raids light the night sky or riding piggyback as their family moves to a refugee camp. Young children can sleep through tornado sirens, thunderstorms, and the loud voices of squabbling older siblings. A mother's arms are all that's required for them to be at peace, to live shalom.

Children live shalom because they have a leaning-weight trust in their parents. Children are powerless, yet they teach us that we too can have a calm and quiet soul precisely *because* someone else is in control. Children teach us that perfect peace, shalom, requires complete surrender. It's out of this place of surrender, this place of leaning-weight wholeness, that they can live boldly.

The peace that Jesus talked often about—the peace that surpasses all understanding, that is utterly incomprehensible to a watching world—is the sort of peace we see in young children as they lean their entire weight on their parents. The Psalms remind us of the blessedness of a leaning-weight trust:

> [The woman who delights in the law of the Lord] will be like
>   a tree *firmly* planted by streams of water,
> Which yields its fruit in its season
> And its leaf does not wither;
> And in whatever [s]he does, [s]he prospers.
> (Psalm 1:3, NASB)

The woman whose hope and confidence is the Lord, the woman who places a leaning-weight trust on Jesus, is like a tree planted firmly by the waters. She spreads forth her roots and her leaves never wither or turn brown. She is not fearful or anxious. She yields fruit in its season, trusting the Lord during seasons of fruitfulness and also during seasons of refreshment and healing, seasons where "fruit" may not be as obvious. She knows there is a time for everything and her soul is content with her season. No matter whether she's facing a sleepless season of diapers or a season of emptying the nest she has so lovingly built, her soul is a "baby content" (Psalm 131:2, MSG), like the littlest among us who leans her whole weight upon a parent. She claims that perfect peace in Jesus, a peace that, like a baby sleeping through an air raid, baffles a watching world. She lives complete; she lives shalom.

RELINQUISHING IDOLS

Of course, when we lean our whole weight upon someone or something, we relinquish our ability to stand on our own. Proverbs 3:5

reminds us of this truth: "Trust in the Lord with all your heart, and do not lean on your own understanding." The *Amplified Bible* highlights this notion of leaning-weight trust: "Lean on, trust in, *and* be confident in the Lord with all your heart *and* mind and do not rely on your own insight *or* understanding" (Proverbs 3:5, AMPC).

This can be a frightening concept.

I think back to my son Blaise, the high-flying toddler. As he gains months and years, he also gains a conception of distance. And with that knowledge comes fear. Recently, when my husband went to toss him in the air, Blaise clung to his arms. The funny thing was, Blaise's own efforts at self-preservation were counterproductive. A half-toss resulted in a tangle of arms and a near fall.

I can relate to Blaise's newly discovered fears. It's difficult for me to lean my whole weight upon anything. As the daughter of an alcoholic, I learned early that it wasn't always safe to depend upon someone; vulnerability was to be avoided. I so often relied (and oftentimes still rely) on my own efforts, knowledge, and perceived ability to control contingencies.

But, like Blaise, my efforts at self-preservation are often counterproductive. They prevent me from relying entirely upon the Lord. My boys are teaching me the principle of Proverbs 3:5-6: that we must trust in the Lord with whole hearts and not rely on our own understanding but submit everything to the Lord. Children illustrate that it is *only* when we lean our whole weight upon the safest someone that we are safe and secure. And that means not leaning our whole weight—or even *some* of our weight—upon our own understanding, strength, or skills. Children show us that perfect peace requires complete surrender.

The Old Testament talks a lot about idols and times when

God's people leaned their weight on something other than Him. Ezekiel 8:12 paints a bleak picture of the nation's idol worship. It tells us that, under cover of darkness, the elders were worshipping at the shrine of their own idols. They had painted pictures and carved images and said to themselves "The LORD does not see us, the LORD has forsaken the land" (Ezekiel 8:12). Now, I've never been tempted to bow down to an object I've made with my own hands, and the idea of worshipping an inanimate cow—even one made out of gold—seems quite strange. Even so, I have something in common with the Israelites.

Thousands of years have passed, but still the innate human desire to worship remains. But who (or what) are we worshipping? When we fail to lean our whole weight upon Jesus, we inevitably lean part of our weight on something or someone else. That these idols have new names does not make them any less destructive. Bowing down to self-reliance, wisdom, power, money, fame, stability, or even well-behaved children, is no better than bowing down to a golden calf. Our more modern god-copies aren't as obviously deity substitutes, but anything that takes the place of reliance on Jesus destroys all the same. When we rely on them, we fail to lean our entire weight on Jesus.

Relying on His Power

The problem of self-reliance is age-old. Isaiah tells the story of an Israel under attack by Assyria (the most powerful nation-state of the day) and of the nation's very human reaction. Terrified, the Israelites scrambled to find a savior, begging Egypt, the other world superpower of the day, for aid. There was only one problem: They forgot to ask the great I Am for help first. In the midst of their terror, they set off for Egypt without inquiring of the Lord. They relied on human might and power, scorning the providence and provision of their Father God.

> "Ah, stubborn children," declares the LORD,
> "who carry out a plan, but not mine,
> and who make an alliance, but not of my Spirit,
> that they may add sin to sin;
> who set out to go down to Egypt,
> without asking for my direction,
> to take refuge in the protection of Pharaoh
> and to seek shelter in the shadow of Egypt!"
> (Isaiah 30:1-2)

But of course, the wings of Pharaoh were no help at all. Like our present-day idols of success, hard work, wealth, productivity, education, or perfect parenting, Egypt offers a false hope. Israel's reliance on her is disastrous.

The contrast between self- and other-reliance and reliance on God is stark. We see in Isaiah a Lord eager to go to battle for His people, a Lord prepared to descend with cloudburst, storm, and hailstones. We see a Lord who promises to defeat the Assyrians, striking terror in their hearts at the mere sound of His voice (Isaiah 30:31).

Yet the Israelites set off to Egypt as fast as their horses could carry them.

Watching the departing, prodigal backs of His children, the Father God is grieved. Even as Israel turns away, the Lord seeks them out. He longs to provide for His people, and He reminds them of their true strength: "In returning and rest you shall be saved; in quietness and in trust shall be your strength" (Isaiah 30:15). God anxiously awaits that return. On that day, He says, there will be no weeping. The light of the moon shall be like the light of the sun, the light of the sun sevenfold, and the Lord shall bind all brokenness. The Lord will be present with His people, and He will bless them.

LISTENING TO GOD

"His mama says hang on." My two-year-old was employing every stay-up-late trick. We had investigated the cross-stitching on his quilt, and his attention had turned to the blanket draped across the rocking chair. A young fox complete with goggles and a long scarf was flying a one-seat airplane.

Elijah: "What's that?"

Me: "A fox flying an airplane."

Elijah: "His mama says hang on."

I laughed out loud. You see, Elijah is a bit of a risk-taker. He's a jump-off-the-stairs, climb-every-stool, swing-on-the-monkey-bars kind of guy. So "be careful" and "hang on" are words he frequently hears. It was only natural that his first thought when confronted with a flying fox was that the fox's mama might be a tad bit concerned about his safety.

"But wait," I hear the Lord whisper, *"there's a lesson here for you too."*

His gentle prompting causes me to wonder how often I ride off to Egypt as fast as my own horses of self-reliance, hard work, and stubbornness will carry me. I think of the times I tackle head-on a pressing problem without first inquiring of the Lord, how often I carry out a plan without first making sure it is *His* plan. How many times have my frantic multitasking efforts drowned out His still, quiet voice? *"Wait, slow down. Seek me first. It is in returning to me and in resting in me that you shall be saved. Quietness and trust are your strength."*

Yet the Lord longs to be gracious to me. My prodigal back does not scare Him away. Though I too often rely on my own strength, or the strength of other people or things, I Am stands at the ready with His majestic voice to fight for me—and for you. When we return to Him, when we lean our whole weight upon Him, we are embraced. Like a small child who clings to her mom, we learn that quietness and trust in Jesus are our strength. When we place all of our trust and hope and identity in Him, when we sit back in our chairs, leaning our whole weight upon Jesus, we become childlike.

The Father Is Always at Work

The counselor teaching our church's parenting class remarked on the significant life event common to every person she had counseled in her career: the moment at which children realize their parents are not perfect. For adolescents and those in their eighties alike, this moment in time was life-defining. It's a moment of broken expectations, disappointment, and the truth that our parents are human.

I've recently seen this moment in the shattered expression of my four-year-old. It was the perfect early summer day when Elijah jumped into the swimming pool fully expecting me to catch him. But he was too far away. Although he was safe in his Puddle Jumper, the painful reality of cold water forced up his nose was too much. With a look of surprise, hurt, and bewilderment, he asked, "Mama, why didn't you catch me?"

Sometimes we ask the same question of God. We wonder where He is during heartbreak and loss. We wonder why He permits tragedy and gives evil the momentary victory when He has the power instantly to make all things right. We feel desperately alone. We look around and wonder with the psalmist, "Why have you forsaken me?" (Psalm 22:1). We ask in four-year-old parlance, "Why didn't you catch me?"

There are no easy answers. I may not ever understand why God permitted certain things in my life, but I am comforted by the certainty that He was there. He is the God who was with me, who saw me and had compassion on me, whose heart broke with every tear. He is the Lord who enters into our suffering. That fateful day when Jesus willingly endured the shame of the cross, He set in motion the day when all will be made right. And He is present with us now, always working on our behalf. He is the King of kings, who has time to wash dishes with a small brokenhearted girl. Dear ones, hear me say this: We are never alone—even if it might feel that way. He is with us always, even when we don't see Him.

It's three in the morning. Time for another nighttime feeding, following on the heels of a day spent walking up and down the stairs in an attempt to quiet the rumbles of a tiny acid-reflux tummy. I soothe my first child back to sleep. Eventually the cries soften. Even then I continue to hold him, transfixed by the tranquility creeping across his face.

And then it hits me. Elijah will not remember this. He will not remember the days of unending tummy aches. He will not remember overeating to soothe his acid reflux. He will not remember me marching up and down the stairs with him during the daytime, a motion that's inexplicably relieving. And he will not remember the nighttime routine—eat, cry, cry some more, and finally sleep—that took place at two-and-half-hour intervals. Even more unsettling: Elijah will not remember the joy with which I hold him at 3:00 a.m.

So much love goes unseen. The clothes get washed and the dishes done after little ones are in bed. Sleep is foregone for a sick toddler or a midnight-talking teenager. (The average mom loses two months' worth of sleep during a baby's first year of life.) Silent prayers are offered up for children morning, noon, and night. Work is attended to in order to provide for little ones' needs or a twenty-year-old's college tuition.

As I consider the sleepless nights of early baby days and the acts of love and service my children may never comprehend, I am undone by this thought: How much of God's love goes unseen? How much do I fail to see the God of the universe at work in my life, providing for all of my needs? Do I comprehend the creation, caretaking, and ultimate sacrifice of a loving heavenly Father? Do I take time to enjoy His blessing and provision?

The efforts of loving parents, valiant as they are, pale in comparison to the unseen acts of divine love. The Father God is *always* working on our behalf. As Jesus tells His disciples, "My Father is working until now, and I am working" (John 5:17). He is the God who never sleeps or slumbers. But there are times when, like my small children, I cannot see His hands reached out in loving provision. There are times when His footprints of love are unseen.

Psalm 77 recounts God's magnificent wall-of-water rescue. The banks of the Red Sea piled high as Israel walked on dry land to escape Egyptian slavery. Yet, amidst one of the most amazing rescues in all of history, the psalmist tells us that the author and architect of that grand plan—the Father God—was not always visible to the Israelites. "Your way was through the sea, your path through the great waters; *yet your footprints were unseen*" (Psalm 77:19, emphasis mine).

Although the Israelites did not see God's footprints, the path to freedom was *God's* path: the path He had prepared and provided. Even when He was unseen, God was leading His people with the gentle hand of a caretaker, a shepherd, a Father determined to bring His children out of slavery and darkness into the broad places of light and life and sovereign protection.

And this was just as He had promised. As early as Genesis 28:15, the Lord proclaimed, "I am with you and will keep you wherever you go, and will bring you back to this land. For I will not leave you until I have done what I have promised you." And, in promising to deliver the Israelites from Egypt, the Lord's words reverberate: "Be strong, courageous, *and* firm; fear not nor be in terror before them, for it is the Lord your God Who goes with you; He will not fail you or forsake you" (Deuteronomy 31:6, AMPC).

My heart hurts with the knowledge that Elijah may never fully realize the depth of a mother's love. Part of me, it's true, would like credit for all of those hours(!), but more than this, I want Elijah to know that he is worth every sleepless minute. I want him to know that any sacrifice pales in comparison to the joy of being his mom. I want him to know how treasured he is. I want his identity to be rooted and grounded in the knowledge that he is fully, deeply, and unconditionally (though imperfectly) loved.

How much more must the Father's heart break when I fail to recognize the vast dimensions of His love for me—the overflowing, abundant, self-sacrificial love of a perfect dad? This Dad delights in me, saying, "This is my beloved daughter in whom I am well pleased." This Dad promises never to leave me; He surrounds me, indwells me even. This Dad made the heavens and earth, provides all that I need, and promises never to let my foot slip. He upholds all who fall, satisfies the desires of every living thing, and is near to all who call on Him. The One who never slumbers is ever vigilant, watching over us constantly as we come and as we go. We are His most treasured possession.

Dear ones, God the Father is at work not only in the grand rescues but also the mundane. When the bondage of sin and the brokenness of the present world overwhelm us, let's not forget that the Father is *always* at work. We need not fear, for we know that He's working for our good. His story is still unfolding—He's orchestrating the most magnificent of victories—and His path always parts the sea, even when His footprints are not seen.

AT WORK ON YOUR BEHALF

A leaning-weight trust doesn't mean sticking your head in the sand. It doesn't mean being naïve. It doesn't mean pretending that life is easy. Let's consider, for example, Sarah, the wife of Abraham and one of our heroes of the faith. Sarah was barren in a world that demanded male heirs. She lived the life of a nomad, continually leaving home, family, friends, and stability. Because of her beauty, she was passed off twice by Abraham as his sister rather than his wife and left to the mercy of those in power. Yet 1 Peter 3:6 tells us that Sarah is to be admired because she did not fear what was *legitimately* frightening.

The truth is that we always have *something* to be afraid of. We live in a broken world, in a creation that groans, and in a time and place where the Kingdom is inbreaking. The Lord already reigns—but darkness has yet to be finally silenced.

Children show us what it looks like to trust in the midst of difficulty. They lean their entire weight on the one who loves them. They do not rely on their own efforts, skills, or ingenuity but on the arms that hold them close. In this way, children show us how to trust our 24-7 God, who is always working on our behalf.

Recently, our family was considering a new venture in my husband's political career. The thought made me sick to my stomach. Literally. We were just getting settled into his current job, and I was loving his predictable schedule after two demanding years of traveling all over the state of Missouri as he sought to serve as its attorney general. The two years he ran for office were full of late nights, unpredictability, and a lot of stress. And we were going to do it all over again?

I woke early one morning, worrying. I began to pray, asking the Lord to change and strengthen my heart if seeking another office was something He had for our family. I called upon the promises of Romans 8:28, praying that the Lord might somehow use all of the unpredictability, instability, and attention for the good of our two small boys. I asked the Lord to work through the circumstances to build and shape the boys into men of character, courage, and conviction. I pleaded with Him to protect them. Ever so slowly, my heart quieted, believing that the Lord could make this new endeavor a good one for our little ones.

"*But wait,*" the Lord gently whispered, "*I can make this new endeavor a good one for you too.*"

The tears came as I was hit with the realization that I'd been expecting the change to be detrimental for me. For sure, the burden of caring for our small children would fall more heavily on me, and I might be called upon to push pause on my own career (again). But as I sat at the Father's feet that morning, He assured me that He intended good for me, too, that this was not a matter of holding my nose and sacrificing but of resting my entire weight upon His love. "Dear daughter," I can hear the Father say, "know that I am for you. I am always at work on your behalf, leading you, guiding you, providing for all of your needs."

Sometimes it's far easier to believe that the Lord is working for good in the lives of others than to live within that knowledge for ourselves. The most common issue observed by one Catholic priest in twenty years of confession was that most Christians did not believe that God actually liked them.[3] They struggled to believe "that God values them, delights in them, suffers for them, is interested in the details of their lives, has a way through particular sins and difficulties for them, and has a calling for them."[4] As biblical scholar David Ford writes, the essential truth that God desires us "is perhaps the hardest truth of any to grasp."[5]

But it is true, dear one. God the Father is delighted with you. He not only loves you, *He likes you.* That truth can change the way we approach our days; we are the beloved daughters of the King,

who is immensely proud of us. He designed you before the founda-
tions of the earth and established work for your hands. He promises
that nothing can thwart His plans for you—plans to give you a
hope and a future. Dear one, He suffered and *died* to have a relationship with you.

So let's trust Him with childlike confidence. That ability to trust
wholly and completely is almost certainly one of the characteristics
Jesus was thinking of when He said that the Kingdom of Heaven
is made up of those who become like little children. As our small
children lean their entire weight upon us, let's remind ourselves that
when we trust in this sort of all-encompassing way, there's no room
for self- or other-reliance. Let's learn from our children that it's in
quietness and trust that we find strength—God's strength.

In the efforts of loving parents we see a glimmer of our Father
God's love for us. We see a Father who's always at work on our behalf, who loves us, likes us, and delights in us. We see a Father who
invites us to sit back, lift our feet off of the floor, take a deep breath,
and lean back in His arms, safe and secure.

Reflection Questions on Trust

1. Take a moment to reflect upon how God is providing for you. In what circumstances could He be working in your life even though you may not see His footprints?

2. Is it difficult for you to lean your entire weight upon Jesus? How might your day be different if you did so?

3. What things do you cling to as a substitute for clinging to God? Stability? Security? Your ability to be flexible or to raise well-behaved children? What would you need to let go of to fully lean upon Jesus? Are there situations in which you need to relinquish control? How might you begin to let go of these things and cling to your heavenly Father instead?

4. Dear one, do you know that the Lord your God likes you? For a reminder, read Zephaniah 3:17.

11

Praise

Let everything that has
*breath praise the L*ORD*!*
—PSALM 150:6

I can remember like it was yesterday. The first halting steps. One, two. And then the beaming face. Elijah was so proud to have walked, to have used a body for upright locomotion that had seemed good only for crawling. His broad smile shared his contagious joy.

Children take joy in the way they are made. They delight to learn new things. They intrinsically know that this trapping we call a body is useful and valuable and something that should give us joy. As they rejoice in their design, they show us how to glorify God with our every going-about-our-day action. Children also invite those closest to them into their achievements, large and small. "Look, Mama, look" is a constant refrain. Children naturally overflow with praise as they invite others to experience delight with them. They show us that joy is incomplete until it is expressed. They show us that praise is the natural response to joy, and that to enjoy God and to praise Him turn out to be the same thing.

Praising God's Design

Elijah is teaching me daily about praising God's design, even when that design comes with weaknesses. Just last month, Elijah was diagnosed with Perthes, a hip disease where the top of the femoral joint dies from lack of blood flow. X-rays revealed the condition: a spherical femur sits comfortably in its right hip socket. On the left side, however, about half of his hip ball joint is missing; it has died and fragmented. The long-term prognosis is good for children his age: Once the blood flow returns, the body will heal itself in most cases (which seems nothing short of a modern-day miracle), but the disease comes with a significant reduction in range of motion and physical activity—something difficult for an active boy.

I am humbled and awestruck as I watch Elijah. Even though his leg is not working like it should, the way his mama desperately wishes it would, Elijah takes delight in how he is made. When he was first diagnosed, he had trouble running per usual, but that didn't slow him down one bit. He could skip. Initially, the doctors had a hard time evaluating him because he insisted on showing them that he could run-skip as fast as ever. As the disease has progressed, Elijah has slowed to a walk on many days. As heartbreaking as this is to his watching mama, Elijah has never once complained. He has never once wished for what he doesn't have—for the movement he used to enjoy so freely. He has never once compared his leg to others.

Elijah is teaching me how to praise God for the way we are made, instead of complaining or comparing. He is once again my tutor as he accepts the way his hip is currently made and maintains a childlike perspective of joy in the many things he can and does do well. With childlike unselfconsciousness, for example, he recently told his Nana and Papa that he was the fastest kid at preschool. And you know, on his good days, I think he just might be telling the truth.

Children are such a good example here. They don't yet know to look in the mirror critically. They don't know that someone else can jump higher and run faster. And they don't care. Children take enormous joy in *their* lives; they don't try to live someone else's. They don't use Facebook or stare longingly at staged vacation pictures. For the childlike, it's not about comparison but enjoyment. They've been given their bodies, and they are bound and determined to figure out their limits. And somehow, even when those limits become very apparent, as with Elijah, they continue to rejoice in their design. As children enjoy the lives that the Lord has given them, they glorify and praise their Father in heaven.

And that's why God created us: so that we might praise Him. In Isaiah, He calls us "the people whom I formed for myself that they might declare my praise" (Isaiah 43:21). The Spirit, in other words, breathed life-breath into our spirits so that we might praise and glorify God. One way we praise and glorify God is to accept and enjoy the way God has made us.

"The aim of having bodies," John Piper has said, "is to make the glory of God more visible."[1] God created you in His own image to dream and work and laugh and love and labor and hope and eat and enjoy the good gifts in this world. Author Tish Harrison Warren expands on this idea: "[I]n the Scriptures we find that the body is not incidental to our faith, but integral to our praise and worship. We were made to be embodied—to experience life, pleasure, and limits in our bodies."[2]

Children show us what it means to praise God by stewarding our bodies well. They take joy in their physical composition. They delight in learning new things. As inches add to their abilities, they rejoice in the newfound capability to reach the light switch, to walk up the stairs without holding your hand, to feed themselves.

We praise and glorify God as we, like a small child, take pleasure in our design, our unique personalities, our giftings, and our strengths. As image-bearers, we bring the Lord glory when we reflect Him. We praise Him by embracing His transformative vision for our lives and when we live in the daughter-identity that He has given us.

For my thirtieth birthday, my amazing friend Sarah put together a "blessing book." She collected letters from family and friends describing various ways in which I had been a blessing to them. Their words are breathtakingly meaningful, incredibly humbling, and sometimes funny.

One of the more unique entries came from Sarah's husband. He wrote that his prayer for me was that I might become "ever more Erin." At first blush, I took slight offense. What did that mean, anyway? That I was somehow less than? That I needed to work harder and become more? But the passage of time has brought the phrase to me over and over again, and those words have now become a prayer of mine. I pray that, like my children, I might become more and more comfortable with the way God has made me; that I would allow Him to mold, shape, and transform me into His vision for me. I pray that, like my children, I won't compare myself to others but fully enjoy the way the Lord has designed me. I pray that I might become ever more Erin.

To do that, I need to be alert. I've realized I sometimes talk to myself in ways that are inconsistent with what God says about who I am. For example, I often catch myself saying "I'm not any good at that" and was recently shocked and convicted by hearing my four-year-old offer the same conclusion about himself. If we don't embrace the way God made us, what are we saying to Him? If He made me more of an introvert and I long to be the most extroverted person in the world, am I missing what God has for me? Am I telling Him that He got it wrong?

Chariots of Fire is one of my favorite movies. In one scene, the famous Scottish missionary Eric Liddell runs. Head thrown back, mouth open wide, arms flailing, Eric is a track coach's nightmare. But he is fast. Olympic gold fast. Talking about his decision to pursue running before becoming a missionary, Eric says, "I believe that God made me for a purpose—for China. But he also made me fast! And when I run, I feel his pleasure."[3] There is no doubt in my mind that no one got more joy from watching Eric run, head flung back and arms flailing, than His Father God.

Dear one, that same Father God takes pleasure in you. He created you for His glory. He created you so that you might praise Him, with your voice and actions and by enjoying every good gift He has given you—including your very design. Just as the Father God took enormous pleasure in watching Eric Liddell run, He takes enormous joy in watching you live *your* life.

Regardless of what we may think of our physical bodies, God looks at us and sees beauty. He sees His creation. He sees His beloved vested with unique talents and gifts. He chose you, just as you are. You are created, redeemed, and indwelled by the Holy Spirit. God thinks you are breathtakingly beautiful, dear one. He numbers the hairs on your head and has made His home in you. We praise Him when we value and care for the bodies He has given us.

The thought that we are, that I am, created to praise and glorify God overwhelms me. How do I even begin?

PRAISING GOD WITH OUR DAILY WORK

With characteristic zest, children show us what it looks like to live a life of praise. They show us how to praise God with our every action. I think of my boys somersaulting down bounce house slides or the stairs in our house (seriously?). Somehow, the sheer terror of it all results in breathless delight. Children push their bodies to the limits. They make full use of their capacities, talents, and gifts; they revel in their ability, even if these things are difficult, to run and to dance.

By living the lives they've been given, by embracing their design and gifts, my boys help me to understand more fully the command of Romans 12:1: to present our bodies as a living sacrifice. Romans 12 tells us that true worship and praise is the devotion of our entire lives to God. As *The Message* puts it, "Take your everyday, ordinary life—your sleeping, eating, going-to-work, and walking-around life—and place it before God as an offering" (Romans 12:1). Children show us how to praise by their exuberant embrace of every undertaking—no matter how small or seemingly insignificant.

A special word here for moms. No task is insignificant. The work that God has given you to do today—nursing your baby, changing diapers, wiping noses and bottoms, cleaning up messes, sweeping the kitchen floor for the umpteenth time—it is *valuable*. The tasks that can seem mundane and monotonous may be the very servantlike ones that the God Most High values most.

As a mom, it can feel as if so much of what you do year-in and year-out goes unseen. It can feel as if no one notices how many diapers you have changed today or how many hours of sleep you have sacrificed. But the God who knows when every sparrow falls counts every minute of sleep you have gone without, every time you've eaten standing up, every time you've been fragile with exhaustion.

You are seen, dear one. And the work you are doing today has immense value.

Under the new covenant, we no longer bring sacrifices to the altar, but our lives *become* the sacrifice. John Piper writes, "It is your *living* that is the act of worship."[4] This understanding of worship and praise transforms the way we see our lives and our work. It isn't just those in full-time ministry who are doing God's work but every one of us in our ordinary lives. When the whole of our lives is offered to God, we can worship Him and bring Him glory through our *every* action.

The famous reformer Martin Luther gave dignity to secular work. He rejected the view that religious activities were the most worshipful but rather argued that it's "a good work when a man works at his trade, walks, stands, eats, drinks, sleeps, and does all kinds of works for the nourishment of his body or for the common welfare."[5] In contrast to those who would define religious good works narrowly—praying, fasting, and almsgiving—Luther emphasized the value God places on ordinary work.[6] In particular, Luther taught that the Lord was especially pleased with the normal things of family life, even though some of those things (like changing diapers!) might seem culturally "insignificant, distasteful, [or] despised."[7]

Centuries later, his namesake, Dr. Martin Luther King Jr., made the same point: "No work is insignificant. All labor that uplifts humanity has dignity and importance and should be undertaken with painstaking excellence."[8]

"If a man is called to be a street sweeper, he should sweep streets even as Michelangelo painted or Beethoven composed music or Shakespeare wrote poetry. He should sweep streets so well that all the hosts of heaven and earth will pause to say, 'Here lived a great street sweeper who did his job well.'"[9]

The Martin Luthers understood the core teaching of Romans 12: We are to offer up the entirety of our lives in praise and worship. We are to hold no part of ourselves back. We are to praise God with our voices, our eyes, our ears, our hands, and our feet. The Romans 12 picture of worship upends our church culture's current definition of praise—as thirty-some minutes of singing before the sermon begins. We are to offer up everything in worship and praise—our time, resources, work, dreams, and ambitions.

As we offer God our lives, the very calling of motherhood becomes praise. Each and every moment placed before God is an offering. And make no mistake: This offering of your everyday life is just as pleasing to the Lord as a well-attended sermon or worship service.

Dear ones, this is such good news. God is satisfied, delighted even, with us and our worship and praise of Him when we offer the lives He has given us—not someone else's life but our very own—back to Him.

PRAISE AS COMPLETED DELIGHT

We were in Colorado enjoying a view of the mountains from the hotel swimming pool when Elijah noticed a gondola traversing the mountain peaks. "Look, look," Elijah shouted. "The gondolas, the gondolas." We had ridden those same gondolas the previous day to the delight of Elijah and his younger brother. Elijah could not contain his excitement. He ran over to Blaise, continuing to shout "Look, look!" He grabbed Blaise's head, cranked it around, and pointed it in the direction of the gondolas (and the bright mountain sun). Elijah's delight was not complete until it was expressed and shared with someone he loved. He could not contain his delight but spontaneously overflowed with praise.

When Jesus speaks to His disciples about becoming childlike, He is likely thinking of young ones' spontaneous outbursts of praise. The smallest delight engenders the most exuberant worship. For children, praise and worship are part of the fun. They complete the enjoyment. For C. S. Lewis, this sort of childlike, spontaneous praise answered for him the question why a self-sufficient God would seek the worship of humans.

> But the most obvious fact about praise—whether of God
> or anything—strangely escaped me. . . . I had never noticed
> that *all enjoyment spontaneously overflows into praise.*
>   I think we delight to praise what we enjoy because the
> praise not merely expresses but completes the enjoyment; it
> is its appointed consummation. It is not out of compliment
> that lovers keep on telling one another how beautiful they
> are; the delight is incomplete till it is expressed.[10]

In the spontaneous praise of the childlike—"Oh, oh, oh, Mama, look, Mama look"—we see the proof of C. S. Lewis's theory: Praise bubbles up spontaneously from enjoyment.

A child's joy, moreover, is incomplete until shared. Children demand an audience for their praises: "Mama, come and see!" They do not rest until those they love most also experience their joy. Children invite you into their delight. As C. S. Lewis observed, "The Psalmists in telling everyone to praise God are doing what all men do when they speak of what they care about."[11] By asking for our praise, God is inviting us to enjoy Him and the world He created for us.

PRAISING WITH CHILDLIKE AWE

Psalm 150:6 reminds us that God designed everything—every animal, every person—with breath to praise Him. In order to praise God for who He is and what He has done for us, we first must open our eyes to see. The awe-filled eyes of a small child show us how to look at our world in a way that gives rise to spontaneous praise.

Luke 5 details one of Jesus' first miracles. It tells us the story of faithful friendship, of men who carried their paralyzed friend to Jesus for healing. When crowds blocked the entryway of the home where Jesus was teaching, these friends dismantled the roof and lowered their friend down to the feet of Jesus. When Jesus saw their faith, He healed their friend instantaneously. As the crippled man stood and walked on once useless legs, those around Jesus were filled with awe. The *Amplified Bible* (Classic Edition) captures their sense of excitement: "And overwhelming astonishment *and* ecstasy seized them all, and they recognized *and* praised *and* thanked God; and they were filled with *and* controlled by reverential fear and kept saying, We have seen wonderful *and* strange *and* incredible *and* unthinkable things today!" (Luke 5:26).

On most any afternoon, children see the extraordinary. They

see "strange and incredible and unthinkable things" every day. One very ordinary Sunday, for example, the rain broke heavy from gray clouds and came pelting down in sheets. The adults in the church foyer let out a collective groan. The skies had been clear when the service started and there was not an umbrella in sight. Then a little joy-filled voice sliced through the sighs. "Let's go play in the rain," my two-year-old exclaimed. The inconveniences of life—wet hair, damp pants, and soggy shoes—simply don't count when you are a kid. Kids take the time to feel the kiss of rain on their faces. They see, and they touch, and they feel. They are so often awestruck. The lit-up face of a toddler displays life at its fullest, at its most abundant. By approaching life with an expectation of awe, small children show us how to more naturally praise God.

This childlike view may place the world in proper perspective. Have you ever returned to a place you loved as a child and been surprised at its smallness? How it diminished in size and grandeur as you grew up and matured? How that restaurant you thought was so special was really a fast-food chain? As we grow up, life can lose some of its sparkle, some of its wonder.

In The Chronicles of Narnia series, the youngest heroine, Lucy, sees Aslan a number of times as she gains years. For her, age has the opposite effect of what we'd expect. Aslan doesn't get smaller; he *grows*. He gets larger with each passing year. For Lucy, God gets bigger each time she sees Him.

When Jesus called the little children to Him, I like to think their starstruck wonder warmed His heart. As we mature, one thing that can help us maintain this sense of awe is the knowledge that God created the world in all of its splendor with us in mind.

Stasi Eldredge tells an encouraging story in *Captivating*. After a particularly rough day, when her marriage was on the rocks and her life in disarray, Stasi stood beneath the vast Colorado sky. She was overwhelmed by the beauty of the heavens. Every star was perfect. And there were so many of them. Then she heard the Lord whisper to her about the splendor surrounding her as to a child: "I'm glad you like it, my darling."[12]

The Bible invites us to "stop and consider the wondrous works of God" (Job 37:14). As we take time to look at the night sky, as we consider all that His hands have made, the good Father reveals Himself and becomes more awesome and wonderful in our eyes as we age.

Max Lucado speculates that even "if you were the only person on earth, the earth would look exactly the same."[13] The Himalayas. The Caribbean. The Rockies. They would all exist in their present splendor because God made all of creation for you and is waiting for you to discover its beauty. He's waiting for the moment when your breath catches to lean forward and whisper, "Do you like it? I did it just for you."[14] The thought overwhelms: All of the earth's beauty was made for us, individually. In inviting us to become childlike, the Father is inviting us to appreciate and enjoy the hues of a sunset or the song of a frog (they really do sing!). He made them with us in mind.

Early mornings help me remember the wonder of childhood. The sun peeks over the horizon, bringing with it a rainbow of pinks, purples, and oranges. As the cascading sunlight strikes blades of frost-covered grass, it reflects sparkles in every direction. When I reflect on mornings like this, when I stand still and absorb the morning sun's rays, when I stop to count the colors of the sky or marvel at the reflecting shimmer of ice-covered-grass glory, I am overcome with awe. The very "heavens declare the glory of God, and the sky above proclaims his handiwork" (Psalm 19:1). As creation itself sings a love song to the one who made it, I am reminded of the glory of the great I Am. All I have to do is stop and look with childlike eyes.

SHARING JESUS THROUGH PRAISE

How beautiful upon the mountains are the feet of him who brings good news. (Isaiah 52:7)

It's easy in this life to focus on achievement: on degrees earned, cases won, awards accepted, money made or saved, or even well-raised children. For the apostle Paul, a man of great learning, position, and prestige—a man who could have been at the top of any achievement pyramid—his crowning accomplishment was the people he introduced to Jesus. They were his hope, joy, and crown. They were his glory (1 Thessalonians 2:19–20). Dear ones, we have the incredible privilege of introducing our children to Jesus.

In the great commission, the Lord commands us to "bring salvation to the ends of the earth" (Acts 13:47). He has made us a light for the world, entrusted us with the good news of His Son Jesus Christ, and sent us out to praise God and to tell of the living hope He offers and of His love for humankind.

As moms, we have the special privilege of sharing Jesus with our little ones. And we can do this through simple, spontaneous acts of praise. Our children are paying attention. This past Christmas season, for example, "Away in the Manger" floated out of our car radio.

"You used to sing that song to me when I was a baby," my four-year-old said.

I smile. "Yes, I did."

Now, his timeline may have been a bit off, but the words brought joy to my heart. Those songs had mattered. Those words had mattered. Those moments mattered. A year later, the memory was still imprinted upon my son's heart. Our children remember when we recognize God for who He is and what He does. They remember when we praise God.

We moms may not be able to see growth in the day-to-day; life gets hectic, sleep gets more precious and patience more difficult, and yet the small moments matter. Precious and lasting are the moments we choose grace and life over harsh words. Precious and lasting are all of the Bible stories, songs, and discussions about Jesus; the times you answer those most honest of toddler questions: "Mom, if Jesus is here, why can't I see Him?" Precious and lasting are the moments when we mess up and our children see us accept grace. How amazing to be the feet of those who get to tell our little ones about Jesus.

Dear one, hear God today. He created you for His glory and to praise Him. And we can praise God simply by offering our everyday lives to Him. As we do so, the very work of mothering our young ones becomes a praise song. As we see our children's spontaneous responses of wonder and awe, let's remind ourselves how praise completes our enjoyment, and that to praise God and to enjoy Him are the same thing. And finally, let's remember that praising Jesus with simple words of gratitude introduces little ears to the one who made the stars and loves them (and us) beyond all measure.

Reflection Questions on Praise

1. What would it look like for you to embrace the way God has made you—including all of your giftings, callings, strengths, and weaknesses? Ask God to help you see yourself the way He does.

2. Are there distractions or habits that keep you from embracing the way God has made you? Does viewing carefully selected images on Facebook, Pinterest, and Instagram lead to unfair comparisons, for example?

3. Is it possible that God might see the day in, day out of the mothering work you do as an incredibly valuable praise offering? Read Romans 12:1 in *The Message*, and offer each activity to God, whether it's changing a particularly smelly diaper, comforting your child, or telling your child about Jesus. Know that you are serving the King of kings.

4. Do you believe that this sort of offering of your ordinary life pleases God? Why or why not? What are some verses or promises of God that might help you? For a reminder, read Genesis 1:31, Zephaniah 3:17, and Jeremiah 32:41.

Conclusion

M y son was up early this morning—too early!—and as I went to tuck him back in, the smell of bad breath from his five-year-old body was shocking. I am often similarly astonished by the smelliness of my boys' feet. The odors of growing up take me by surprise. But this morning, they also cause in me a vast sense of wonder. The tiny boys who could rest in one arm and were content to nap the day away snuggled close have become preschoolers who bound and leap and explore their growing independence—and yes, sometimes stink. They will one day become men who work and worship and provide.

The miracle of the human body strikes me anew this morning with that whiff of bad breath. It's an incredible gift to see the divine process of growth—a process that not only reveals but also reflects the very image of God. Part of God's gift for me in my children's early years has been seeing the childlike in them.

As moms, we have a front-row seat to the miraculous unfolding of God's design for humankind. It's no accident, dear one, that God has given you your particular children—for their benefit and yours. He plans and names every family on earth. And in addition to caring for your beautiful little ones as no one else can do, He's given an additional purpose to motherhood: to show us how to live as beloved children of God.

Mark tells us that Jesus was indignant when His disciples turned the children away. Instead, He bid them to come near. Jesus scooped the children up in His arms, placed His hands on them, and blessed them (Mark 10:16). Dear ones, as you move through your day today, as you go about the vital work of nurturing your own children, go to God as His child. Let Him scoop you up and hold you close. As you rest in His arms with childlike vulnerability and trust, feel His presence. Let Him place His hands upon you and bless you. You are His.

I pray that through our journeys as moms, we would see Jesus pull our children close and delight in them, and remember that in the same way, He pulls us close and delights in us too. I pray that, like our children, we will come to fully know and fully experience the comfort, joy, confidence, courage, rest, and hope-filled anticipation of a life lived beloved—that we would learn to become childlike.

Acknowledgments

As with anything worthwhile, this book is the product of countless hands and prayers—many of them extended in grace years before the first word was written.

Josh, thank you for your faith in me. You are always much more certain of the value of my work than I am. Thank you for encouraging and building me up in this journey of motherhood. I am so grateful to be on this adventure of life with you. We all adore you.

Victoria, Jenny, Lana, Bridget, Jessie, Haley—thank you for being my "Bible study girls." Thank you for graciously studying the first draft of this book and for convincing me that the lessons I am learning from my kiddos might encourage other moms too. Thank you for the prayers for my family and for this book. Most of all, thank you for sharing your life with me. I am so grateful for your friendship. I love you guys.

Kristi, Tamara, Grace, Victoria, and Dee Dee, thank you for being my constants in an ever-changing world of seasons: new homes, new babies, new callings. Thank you for laughing with me and crying with me, for lifting me and those I love up in prayer, and for praying when I don't know how. Thank you for knowing me at my worst, yet seeing in me the best. Thank you for always reaching out—for being for me the hands and feet of Jesus. It's a privilege to live life together, dear ones. Love to you.

Sharie and Diane, thank you for being my home away from home.

Ron, Ginni, and Leslie, thank you for loving me as your own and being an unyielding source of encouragement.

Thank you to my sisters, Maggie and Rori, who know me best and somehow love me still. And who graciously allowed me to share part of their story in these pages. I am amazed by you both and love you beyond measure.

Mom, thank you for always pointing me to Jesus. I marvel more every day at your constant love, correction, and wisdom. How did you do it? Your efforts astound me! I know that one day you will receive your reward. With trumpet blast and much fanfare, the Jesus who has seen your every sacrifice will applaud your life of faithfulness. All that I have are the insufficient words *thank you*.

Finally, thank you to my awesome editor, Julie Holmquist, and the fabulous team at Focus on the Family. It has been a blessing to work on this project with you.

About the Author

Erin Hawley is a wife, mom to two small boys, and some-time lawyer. She is also an award-winning law professor at the University of Missouri, Yale-trained constitutional lawyer, and counsel attorney to one of the country's premier law firms.

Erin clerked for United States Supreme Court Chief Justice John G. Roberts following law school. She is a nationally respected scholar who has published in numerous top law journals and popular publications, including the *National Law Journal*, the *Legal Times*, the *Federalist*, the *Hill*, *Fox News*, and the *Washington Examiner*. In addition, Erin is a frequent radio and television commentator, and routinely speaks to large audiences all over the country.

Erin has been blessed to work primarily from home since the birth of her first child and is intimately familiar with the joys and struggles of working-mom life. She loves coffee-flavored lattes (but not coffee), being outside in the sunshine, horses and dogs, facilitating Bible studies, and fellowship with other women.

Notes

Chapter 1: Humble Imitation

1. Sally Lloyd-Jones, *The Jesus Storybook Bible: Every Story Whispers His Name* (Grand Rapids, MI: ZonderKidz, 2007), 37.
2. Beth Moore, *Breaking Free: Discover the Victory of Total Surrender* (Nashville: B&H Publishing Group, 2007), 2.
3. http://www.kristinschell.com/the-prayer-of-st-patrick/

Chapter 2: Living Beloved

1. As quoted by Violet Bonham Carter in *Winston Churchill as I Knew Him* (1965), according to *The Yale Book of Quotations* (2006), Fred R. Shapiro, Yale University Press, 155.

Chapter 3: Living All-In

1. June Hunt, *Bonding with Your Child through Boundaries* (Wheaton, IL: Crossway, 2015), 21-22 (describing study).
2. Ray Pritchard, *An Anchor for the Soul: Help for the Present, Hope for the Future* (Chicago: Moody Publishers, 2011), 156.
3. Eugene H. Peterson, *Run with the Horses: The Quest for Life at Its Best* (Downers Grove, IL: InterVarsity Press, 2009), 14.

Chapter 4: Transparency

1. John Swinton, *Raging with Compassion: Pastoral Responses to the Problem of Evil* (Grand Rapids, MI: William B. Eerdmans Publishing Company, 2007), 115.
2. Ibid.
3. Stanley Hauerwas, *God, Medicine, and Suffering* (Grand Rapids, MI: William B. Eerdmans Publishing Company, 1994), 80.
4. Walter Brueggemann, *The Message of the Psalms: A Theological Commentary* (Minneapolis: Augsburg Publishing House, 1984), 52.

5. Ibid.
6. Hauerwas, *God, Medicine, and Suffering*, 82.
7. Brueggemann, *The Message of the Psalms: A Theological Commentary*, 51.
8. Hauerwas, *God, Medicine, and Suffering*, 82.
9. Brueggemann, *The Psalms and the Life of Faith* (Minneapolis: Fortress Press, 1995), 100.
10. Kirsten Weir, "The Lasting Impact of Neglect," (American Psychological Association, June 2014 Vol. 45. No. 6), 36, available online at http://www.apa.org/monitor/2014/06/neglect.aspx
11. Hauerwas, *God, Medicine, and Suffering*, 82.
12. Swinton, *Raging with Compassion: Pastoral Responses to the Problem of Evil*, 98.
13. Ibid.
14. Ann Weems, *Psalms of Lament* (Louisville, KY: Westminster John Knox Press, 1995), 1-2. Used by permission.

Chapter 5: Embracing Fellowship

1. Henry Cloud and John Townsend, *How People Grow: What the Bible Reveals about Personal Growth* (Grand Rapids, MI: Zondervan, 2004), 120.
2. Ibid.
3. Ibid.
4. Mother Teresa, *A Simple Path* (New York City, NY: Ballantine Books, 1995), 79.
5. Ann Swindell, *Still Waiting: Hope for When God Doesn't Give You What You Want* (Carol Stream, IL: Tyndale House Publishers, 2017), 108-9.
6. Dietrich Bonhoeffer, *Life Together: The Classic Exploration of Christian Community* (San Francisco: HarperOne, 2009), 30.
7. Ibid.
8. Scot McKnight, *The Real Mary: Why Protestant Christians Can Embrace the Mother of Jesus* (Brewster, MA: Paraclete Press, 2016), 8-14.

9. In Mark 6:3, for example, the people of Nazareth referred to Jesus as the "son of Mary," instead of the traditional, "son of Joseph." Scot McKnight identifies this as a slur on Jesus identity. Ibid., 106. Similarly, in John 8:41 the Jews told Jesus "We are not born of sexual immorality" suggesting that Jesus might be.

10. John MacArthur, *The MacArthur New Testament Commentary*, Matthew 8-15 (Chicago: Moody Publishers, 1987), 80.

Chapter 6: Rest

1. Tish Harrison Warren, *Liturgy of the Ordinary: Sacred Practices in Everyday Life* (Downers Grove, IL: InterVarsity Press, 2016), 150.

2. Ibid.

3. Kate Shellnutt, "God Wants You to Get Some Sleep" (*Christianity Today*, January 2017), available at https://www.christianitytoday .com/women/2017/january/god-wants-you-to-get-some-sleep.html

4. Warren, *Liturgy of the Ordinary: Sacred Practices in Everyday Life*, 144.

5. Henri J. M. Nouwen, *Out of Solitude: Three Meditations on the Christian Life* (Notre Dame, IN: Ave Maria Press, 2004), 13.

6. Shellnutt, "God Wants You to Get Some Sleep."

7. D. A. Carson, *Scandalous: The Cross and Resurrection of Jesus* (Wheaton, IL: Crossway, 2010), 147.

8. Warren, *Liturgy of the Everyday: Sacred Practices in Ordinary Life*, 152.

9. Brady Boyd, *Addicted to Busy: Recovery for the Rushed Soul* (Colorado Springs, CO: David C. Cook, 2014), 198.

10. Ibid., 72.

11. D. A. Carson, ed., *From Sabbath to Lord's Day: A Biblical, Historical, and Theological Investigation* (Eugene, OR: Wipf and Stock, 1999), 34-35 (quoted in Brady Boyd, *Addicted to Busy: Recovery for the Rushed Soul.*)

12. Mark Buchanan, *The Rest of God: Restoring Your Soul by Restoring Sabbath* (Nashville: Thomas Nelson, 2007), 88-90.

13. Ibid., 90.

Chapter 7: Bold Requests

1. C. H. Spurgeon, "Ask and Have," a sermon at http://www.spurgeon gems.org/vols28-30/chs1682.pdf Metropolitan Tabernacle Pulpit, October 1, 1882.

2. Mark Batterson, *The Circle Maker: Praying Circles around Your Biggest Dreams and Greatest Fears* (Grand Rapids, MI: Zondervan, 2016), 17.

3. *Hymns Ancient & Modern Ltd.* (London, 2013), "Prayer Is the Soul's Sincere Desire," James Montgomery, #767.

Chapter 8: Limitless Joy

1. C. S. Lewis, *Surprised by Joy: The Shape of My Early Life,* (New York: HarperOne, reissue edition, 2017).

2. Gordon D. Fee, *Paul's Letter to the Philippians* (Grand Rapids, MI: William B. Eerdmans Publishing Company, 1995), 404.

3. John Piper, "Jesus's Pursuit of Joy," September 24 Devotional available at https://www.desiringgod.org/articles/jesus-s-pursuit -of-joy

4. Lisa Bevere, *Without Rival: Embrace Your Identity and Purpose in an Age of Confusion and Comparison* (Grand Rapids, MI: Revell, 2016), 163.

5. *Oxford Advanced American Dictionary* (Oxford University Press, 2011).

6. Jeroen Nawijn, et al., *Vacationers Happier, But Most Not Happier After Holiday*, Appl Res Qual Life. March 2010; 5(1): 35–47. Abstract available at: https://www.ncbi.nlm.nih.gov/pmc/articles /PMC2837207/

7. *Strong's Concordance* (Nashville, TN: Thomas Nelson, 2010).

8. A. W. Tozer, *Evenings with Tozer,* April 30 (Chicago, IL: Moody Publishers, 2015).

9. Ibid.

10. Henri J. Nouwen, *Out of Solitude: Three Meditations on the Christian Life* (Notre Dame, IN: Ave Maria Press, 2004), 14.

Chapter 9: Lean Up

1. Joanna Barsh, "Facebook's Sheryl Sandberg: 'No one can have it all,'" April 2013, https://www.mckinsey.com/business-functions/organization/our-insights/facebooks-sheryl-sandberg-no-one-can-have-it-all
2. Sheryl Sandberg, *Lean In*, (New York: Alfred A. Knopf, 2013), 38.
3. Nicky Gumbel, *The Bible in One Year*, 2017, Day 146, https://www.bible.com/reading-plans/3420-bible-in-one-year-2017/day/146

Chapter 10: Trust

1. Nicky Gumbel, *The Bible in One Year*, 2017, Day 146, https://www.bibleinoneyear.org/bioy/commentary/1435
2. Ibid.
3. David F. Ford, *The Shape of Living: Spiritual Directions for Everyday Life*, (Grand Rapids, MI: Baker Books, 2004), 59.
4. Ibid.
5. Ibid.

Chapter 11: Praise

1. John Piper, *Present Your Bodies as a Living Sacrifice to God*, June 13, 2004, http://www.desiringgod.org/messages/present-your-bodies-as-a-living-sacrifice-to-god
2. Tish Harrison Warren, *Liturgy of the Ordinary: Sacred Practices in Everyday Life* (Downers Grove, IL: InterVarsity Press, 2016), 152.
3. *Chariots of Fire* (1981), https://www.youtube.com/watch?v=Pd5LCN53q9Y, accessed May 4, 2018.
4. Piper, *Present Your Bodies as a Living Sacrifice to God*.
5. Martin Luther, cited in Ian Hart, *The Teaching of Luther and Calvin about Ordinary Work*, *Evangelical Quarterly* 67, No. 1, 1995, 36, https://biblicalstudies.org.uk/pdf/eq/1995-1_035.pdf.
6. Ibid., 35-37.
7. Ibid., 37.

8. The King Center, http://www.thekingcenter.org/blog/mlk-quote-week-all-labor-uplifts-humanity-has-dignity-and-importance-and-should-be-undertaken

9. Ibid.

10. C. S. Lewis, *Reflections on the Psalms* (New York: HarperOne, reprint edition, 2017), 109.

11. Ibid., 109-110.

12. John and Stasi Eldredge, *Captivating* (Nashville: Thomas Nelson, 2010), 113.

13. Max Lucado, *The Great House of God* (Nashville: W Publishing Group, 1997), 45.

14. Ibid.

Meet the rest of the family

Expert advice on parenting and marriage . . .
spiritual growth . . . powerful personal stories . . .

Focus on the Family's collection of inspiring, practical resources can help your family grow closer to God—and each other—than ever before. Whichever format you need—video, audio, book, or e-book—we have something for you. Discover how to help your family thrive with books, DVDs, and more at **FocusOnTheFamily.com/resources**.

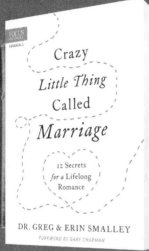